Updated and Expanded 2nd Edition

THE DIGITAL PLAN

STRATEGIC GUIDANCE AND PLANNING TO:

Win political campaigns
Grow nonprofit organizations
Launch projects and meet goals

BRAD A. SCHENCK

Published 2018
Printed in the United States of America
ISBN-13: 978-0692102565 (Custom Universal)
ISBN-10: 0692102566
Library of Congress Control Number: 2018904127

Cover and logo design by Gloria Pak
Interior design by Tabitha Lahr

For information, address: The Digital Plan, 1130 Broadway Suite 300,
Oakland, CA 94612

CONTENTS

WHY THIS BOOK:
LETTER FROM THE EDITOR

Welcome to the digital frontier and congratulations on taking this step toward digital empowerment!

This book is (first and foremost) a labor of love. Brad and I are passionate community-builders using digital strategy to do a wide variety of work—everything from website building to political campaigning, video production, full digital branding packages and more. Over the years, we've learned a LOT, and we've cultivated a strong community of digital do-gooders.

Our community is made up of passionate professionals working as contractors, activists, executives for nonprofits, political campaigners, and more—we can never work fast enough, which is why we made, The Digital Plan. This book will help you navigate digital work and craft a digital plan, inclusive of all experience levels and industries.

We believe the strength of digital strategy is in organizing and integrating diverse voices, which is why this edition includes over 30 case studies, anecdotes, and tips from CEO's, activists, and some of the leading digital strategists across various industries. We've expanded this edition to include new chapters on The Engagement Cycle and SMS, and this edition is also redesigned to make your learning experience as effortless as possible.

This book will evolve and change as technology does, so we hope you join our online community for facilitated conversations, the most up-to-date strategies, and resources to answer your burning questions.

You may be wondering : What is a digital plan, why do I need one and how do I use it?

The digital landscape is both vast and volatile, and it can often be a pain in the ass. We all have a lot of work to do, and keeping up with platforms, strategies, algorithms, and best practices really can be a full-time job, but it doesn't have to be.

Imagine, YOU, empowered.

Take this book. Skim it, read it and love it. Though there is no easy answer to digital strategy, this book is an easy bridge to build your expertise so that you can succeed. Whether you want to "talk the talk" as a techie or if you want to "walk the walk," this book will strengthen your ability to do digital work, well.

There's no such thing as a fixed digital plan which will become clear in The Engagement Cycle chapter. The most important thing is that you know how to read the landscape and navigate through it, and this book will help you do just that.

May you be empowered to amplify your message, movement, and impact. One person can change the world, and an organized digital community can move mountains.

Thank you for joining our community, and please get involved with our online activities with free training options, dynamic conversations and like-minded folks on the digital frontier!

All the best on your digital journey,

Katrina Mendoza

# HOW TO USE THIS BOOK

Welcome to The Digital Plan!
This book is not a "read and done" sort of book; it is a tool that is meant to accompany you through excellent strategic thinking, to leverage digital marketing, engagement, advertising, and technology to win political campaigns, grow nonprofits, and launch successful projects. How you use this tool will likely vary depending on what you are doing for your organization or project.

Let's build some foundation together.

The disciplines that makeup "Digital Departments" or "Digital" titles are often wildly different disciplines that never would have made sense as one team before, and that is part of the struggle. Graphic design, web development, social media, email campaigning, data and analytics, and project management are really, really different disciplines. Most videographers and designers haven't taken a web development course, and most analytics professionals have never taken a design course.

The chapters for these disciplines that make up good digital plans don't follow a formulaic chapter design that may be familiar to you. Instead, you'll get chapters that strategically present practical knowledge, theory, and skills to help you understand that specific discipline.

You might not need to read every chapter, but you should read the **Goals** and **The Digital Planning Engagement Cycle** chapters to get a solid foundational base. Those two chapters are fundamental to what follows. As for the rest of the sections, not every project plan needs web development or video, so read that chapters that you need when you need them. Dog ear some pages, take notes in the margins and join some of the online webinars to drive your strategy to the next level.

How to use this book if you are a manager or in a leadership position.

If you've found yourself in a position of leadership or management where you need to make sense of digital and tech, this book is for you. You might not need to read every chapter or case study. The book will help you get a robust framework for the underlying strategy and challenges of digital and tech.

When approaching new projects, you should read relevant chapters during the planning and execution phases. You'll be able to ask better questions, make more strategic decisions, and help your team design better goals. Throughout the different sections, we'll refer to this cohort as "Non-Digital Leadership or Management."

How to use this book if you are a digital or tech staffer.

The author and many of the contributors have been through the challenges you might be about to face. A real challenge we all face every day is the expectation that, if you work in digital or tech, you know all things digital or tech. Take a big sigh of relief because no-one who knows this field well thinks that is true, and that's why we are investing our energy in this book. None of us alone could be the experts of all of these disciplines.

If you are working in one field of digital and tech, we highly encourage you to read all of the chapters and get to know the struggles of other areas. They all have their nuances and ever-expanding challenges. You are at the forefront of new ways of engaging, empowering, and creating change. Even those of us experienced "old hands" often have that feeling.

As you grow in your role, make sure to invest in goals and the engagement cycle. And as you move from chapter to chapter in this book, think about how the elements move through the engagement cycle themselves to create a tapestry of tasks, engagement, and feedback. Throughout the sections in the book, we'll refer to this cohort as "Digital/Tech Staffers."

How to use this if you're new to digital or tech or an activist trying to leverage it.

Drinking from a firehose is hard. You don't have to become an expert overnight. This book and its companion courses can help you ease into complex information. You can start by skimming the book and leaning more into the case studies and anecdotes to help paint a picture. Then let yourself roll back through the chapters as you are working on projects.

   The book is designed to help you ease your way in and jump around as needed. It wasn't intended for a one-size-fits-all campaign, nonprofit, or project. So evaluate as you go as to what is possible with your project. Throughout the sections, we'll refer to this cohort as "New Staff/Activists."

 # INTRODUCTION

For the five or so years before writing the first edition of this book, I've received emails every few weeks with a request for a digital plan template. My response is, often, that there aren't great one-stop plans and to date, I've written and coached others to draft hundreds of digital projects. The reason is, it depends on what the goals are. As you might imagine, the digital plan for the following purposes look pretty different:

- *Is your goal to launch a video or book?*
- *Is your goal to recruit people to an event?*
- *Is your goal to register people to vote?*

There are overlapping elements with these goals, but without knowing the specific goals and resources of your project, a template without guidance would likely lead you astray because it would contain unnecessary elements. Every time I receive a request for a model, I tell people I care about that it wouldn't be right for me to send a plan from another project because it won't get you what you need. It is because there are so many issues that I care about and too little of my time to go around that I'm writing this book.

The goal of this book is to empower people like you to make informed decisions and insightful plans that advance your mission. It's designed to give you the proper knowledge to ask the right questions, apply planning best practices, and draft your own plan that achieves the goals you want.

A Story About Planning in the 2012 Democratic Primaries

It's 1:30 AM on a weeknight in January 2012. I've just closed my laptop, and I'm trying to fall asleep, but my phone is ringing. It's the Digital Director from Nevada—I groggily ask what's going on and why the call at 1:30 AM. For a few weeks, my mind has been bouncing between Eastern, Central, and Western time zones for the states I'm supporting and my Chicago home; South Carolina, Florida, and Nevada all have a primary or caucus this month.

Primaries and caucuses work different from state to state which may have become very clear in the 2016 election cycle. In every state, it works a little differently, and the dates are set between the political parties and the legislature. In many states, the two parties do not represent primary or caucus on the same day. So we were looking at a South Carolina Republican Primary, Nevada Democratic caucus, and Florida Republican primary. In none of these states would Republicans and Democrats share the same day. I am just back from South Carolina, so my internal clock is telling me it's actually 2:30 AM.

Again, why am I being called? As it turns out, it has something to do with a flyer that the director can't edit and also can't reach his designer. I'm massaging my temples. South Carolina had been a terrible slog of meetings and planning. You might be curious knowing that Democrats don't typically campaign to win South Carolina. It would be fair to ask why we were there focusing on a Republican primary. It simply was part of a broader strategy that involved building energy in South Carolina and translating that into engagement in North Carolina. So I am short to the point in this discussion: "You need to figure this out. It's almost 2 AM here." With push back, I am struggling to grasp what the expectation of this call really is. There is a help center for the Adobe product he is struggling with. I tell him to work on it, and I'll talk to him in the morning.

Moral of this story: We were in this position because this director didn't have a plan. The Director hadn't started with the goals around the caucus and worked backward to determine what would be needed to get there. It was a day-to-day frazzled series of actions, and when you operate that way, you find yourself without the systems you need to get things done in a reasonable way.

If you are reading this, you've probably found yourself in one of several positions. You are in direct control of an organization's communications, you are part of a digital team, or you are driving a project, and you need a plan. You'll also find this handy if you are a leader within an organization or company and want to know where to begin or which questions to ask to make sure your organization is on track. Whether you're on a small campaign, in an organization or simply need to figure this digital business out, in the pages that follow, here is what you will find:

- Guidance and thoughtful questions you should ask.
- Bullet points and lots of them. Planning should at least be succinct.
- Templates that will help you frame your plan.
- Guidance and anecdotes from someone who has helped write and offered advice on hundreds of digital plans.

There is no substitute for intentional planning which is why one-size-fits-all templates don't truly work. This means there are a few things you won't find in this book:

- A silver bullet to success.
- Exact directions on how to use Twitter, Facebook, or any other digital tool, because every organization is different and the tools will change by the time this gets in your hands.
- A plan you can take and just plug your organizational name into.

The chapters that follow walk you through a number of areas that are often rolled into digital departments or digital plans. Depending on the scale of your project or organization, ownership of these elements may live in other departments. For the purpose of this book, we've laid out the chapters to give you the building blocks for a holistic and strategic digital plan. Each chapter can be read on its own or as a building block for a broader plan. We've left margins wide enough for some notes in the print version because we hope you use this book as an ongoing reference for your work.

This book works well with expanded trainings and updated resources offered online at: www.TheDigitalPlan.com. We look forward to building out resources and further tips there. Be sure to stop by and sign-up for updates to get the latest in digital strategy for political campaigns, nonprofits, and projects. With the chapter by chapter building blocks and templates, you should be well on your way to creating a strategic digital plan and making a positive change in the world.

THE DIGITAL PLANNING ENGAGEMENT CYCLE

The Digital Planning Engagement Cycle is critical to healthy digital campaigns that meet goals and drive real engagement. The Engagement Cycle is about the union of goals, tactics, execution, and reflection. Each of the five phases of the Engagement Cycle is a key piece, and it's important not to be hasty because the phases function together as a complete cycle that can build on itself, growing stronger for longer campaigns and projects.

How to use this chapter

This chapter is for everyone. Too often, organizations and campaigns create a plan then don't think of it as a living document that links to ongoing engagement with supporters.

We'll move through the steps of The Digital Planning Engagement Cycle (Engagement Cycle for short) and explain how the milestones are each part of a strategic feedback loop. You should work to make this Engagement Cycle part of ALL of your planning.

KEY TAKEAWAYS AND ELEMENTS:
- A foundational understanding of what the Engagement Cycle is
- Detailed examples of what goes into the phases
- How to use the Engagement Cycle in your planning

The five phases of The Digital Planning Engagement Cycle are as follows:
- Brainstorm & Planning
- Execute
- Engage
- Impact
- Feedback

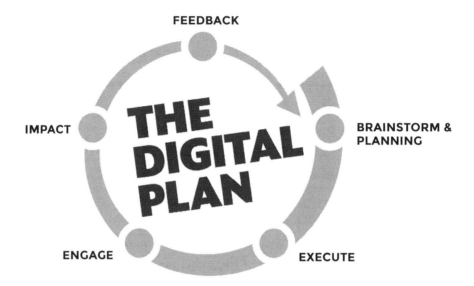

When working on long-term projects, hitting the Feedback milestone should loop back around and influence your new Brainstorming & Planning phase.

Through each section of the book, we'll highlight tips on how to engage in the planning cycle for each tactical discipline. Here is a look more deeply at each of the five phases.

Brainstorm & Planning

In the beginning, we need to identify the goals, allow space for brainstorming to translate the goals to tactics, and lay the foundation for how we'll execute the project.

Brainstorming and planning are combined together as one section because of their inherently connected nature. Even when people aren't holding a formal "brainstorm," they often go through micro-brainstorming flows when they are working through ideas on their own, or over a planning call, or small meeting. Hopefully, in these large and small brainstorms, you are clarifying what your goals are and sorting through the tactics that will help you meet those goals. In the chapters that follow, we'll break down helpful tips on how different tactics can be used to reach your goals. It's important to first recognize brainstorming as a phase for clarifying goals before we can dig into different tactics for achieving goals.

The brainstorming phase is where we allow ourselves to get creative and think through how we'll tackle a challenge before distilling it into a plan and then bringing it to life through the rest of the Engagement Cycle. The key to a successful brainstorm is to remain focused on what it is you want to do, and who you want to do it for.

As you go between brainstorming and planning there are several essential elements you need to think about:
- Goals
- Tactics
- Audiences
- Targets

GOALS: What are you trying to impact in the world and the milestones to get you there.
- There is an entire chapter dedicated to helping establish goals.

TACTICS: How you are going to reach your goal.
- You might have lots of small tactical goals as well but don't confuse your tactics for goals.
- The entire rest of the book is really about how tactics help meet goals IE using email to meet your goals, web development to meet your goals, design to meet your goals, etc.

AUDIENCES: Who you are trying to reach to move your goals.
- Sometimes your audience is your target, and sometimes they are separate.
- Audiences are part of reaching your goal when you are asking people to sign a petition to persuade an elected official or company.
- Audiences can be the targets for items like fundraising.

TARGETS: Who or what you intend to impact to make a change in the world.
- This can be your supporters directly for a thing like a donation, could be an institution you want to make a change, and elected officials or body, or corporate leader or company at large.

You'll find the master Digital Project Plan and training on the website. www.The-DigitalPlan.com

The design of that planning template is all about laying out a timeline for the main tasks that move you to your goal.

Execute

The creation of needed items, meetings, and tasks to complete tactics.
- Execute is the task phase. Sure it might involve more calls and planning but here is where you are doing the task-based items to bring your plan to life. Things like:
- Drafting emails, blogs, social media, and website copy.
- Designing memes, images for blogs and emails,
- Scripting, filming, editing videos.
- Building, testing, refining websites.

During most plans Execution and Engage start to overlap when emails get sent, text messages are sent and replied to, memes are published social media. Then small feedback loops should start to loop back through engage and execute.

Examples of small feedback loops:

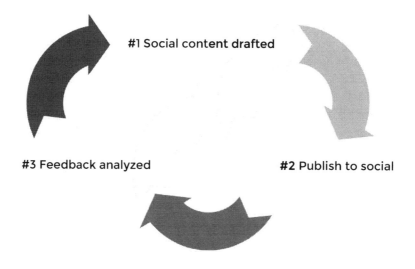

#1 Social content drafted

#3 Feedback analyzed

#2 Publish to social

This is different from the "Feedback" phase, more below.

Engage

Where tactics begin to meet with the targeted audience, often overlapping with execution.

This is the point in the cycle where people see your planned content, emails are being opened, and text messages are showing up on people's phones. Rarely does all of the engagement happen at once. More often than not, it takes over a week to several weeks of a project or targeted campaign to engage audiences.

Email engagement during the Engage phase might be a series of emails over weeks or months and could include things like:

- The initial sign on or sign up form or petition.
- A "thank you for signing" that follows immediately,
    - But remember that this is actually staggered. You are likely asking people to keep signing up for weeks via email, social media, or ads.
- A next step for what they can do.
- The next step.
- Maybe a report back on how things are going.
- Maybe a next step.
- A final close to the campaign or project.

As noted before, small bits of feedback will be cycling back into how you execute. This means if what you are doing is performing poorly, it may be time to change tactics a bit as you understand how your intended engagement is connecting with your audience.

Impact

Understand how the series of actions or content moved the intended audiences, targets, and the goals.

The impact is different from engaging because engagement is an action for the audience you need to move the goal. The impact is focused on the larger goal itself. This often gets cloudy for folks, and there are a few exceptions where it might be very close to the same thing. You can't determine your impact if you don't have concrete goals established back in the Brainstorm and Planning phase.

Here are some examples:

1. If your big goal is to get local legislation or a school board policy change, you would be looking to IMPACT the officials of those bodies, but you would need to ENGAGE your email list to send them a message.

2. If your goal is to raise awareness about climate change, your goal is to IMPACT the net conversation of a topic possibly defined by shares or views online. You would be looking to ENGAGE your social media followers and email list to both watch and share driving your ultimate goal of awareness.

3. If your goal is to raise money for your organization the IMPACT is the funds raised. To do this, you must ENGAGE people with tactics. This is one of the few places where it does blur because the people you wish to ENGAGE are closely associated with the goal for IMPACT.

4. If your goal is to contact voters, your IMPACT is how many voters engaged, and if your tactic was a door to door canvass, then the audience you likely wanted to ENGAGE is your email list and social media following. The success of that ENGAGEMENT is tracked by sign-ups, and the question then is, how did that IMPACT the goal of actually talking to voters?

This nuance matters because your ENGAGEMENT can be great but might not hit the IMPACT you wish. If you have an amazing email list 5,000 people, who open 50% of the emails and 100% of the folks who open 2,500 people make a phone call to their congressperson that might still not be the IMPACT you need if the goal is to change federal legislation.

Feedback

A moment of deeper analysis of what worked, what didn't, and how that impacts future planning or re-engagement around the current goals. Ideally a blend of qualitative and quantitative analysis.

Real feedback is a good blend of quantitative and qualitative analysis that helps you answer questions about what worked, what didn't, what to do less of, what to do more of, and maybe what to test again. This isn't just what was the open rate on an email, or how many views did a video get, or sign-ups to do a thing. Feedback is what can we infer from those numbers, and what kind of impact we actually had on our goals.

Sometimes the Feedback moment has minor impacts on the next round of Brainstorm & Planning. If you are on track and hitting goals, you may just choose to stay on a similar course, and that's okay.

You may come to realize one of your tactics didn't have the engagement you hoped, or even that engagement didn't have the impact on key goals you had planned on. This is where you need to understand if you need to change tactics, build infrastructure, a larger following, or some other milestone for achieving the impact you want.

There is no silver bullet to answer what works and what doesn't. Every campaign, nonprofit, and project is different, but the following chapters and online trainings will help you understand what it means to set and track goals, choose tactics strategically, and build a plan using this cycle.

Summary

The digital planning engagement cycle is critical to meet your goals and drive real engagement. The five phases of the cycle are Brainstorm & Planning, Execute, Engage, Impact and Feedback. Long-term projects mean a more dynamic engagement cycle, and it is an ongoing movement from one phase to the next. Use the Brainstorm & Planning phase to identify the goals, allow space for brainstorming to translate the goals to tactics—this will lay the foundation for the project. The Execution phase includes the creation of needed items, meetings and asks to complete tactics. The Engage phase is where tactics begin to meet with the targeted audience, which will often overlap with the Execution phase. The Impact phase is for understanding how your actions moved the intended audiences, targets, and goals. The Feedback phase is for more in-depth analysis of what worked, what didn't, and how that impacts future planning or re-engagement. Ideally, you will have a blend of qualitative and quantitative analysis.

 # GOALS

At its core, this is a book about Goals. How to ask the right questions to pick the right goals. How to make a plan to get to those goals.

How to use this chapter

This chapter is for everyone. Goals should be the foundation of any solid plan.

This chapter breaks down how to think about different digital goals and one of the biggest struggles in digital planning: The difference between GOALS and TACTICS.

KEY TAKEAWAYS AND ELEMENTS:
- Goals—Why you need them
- How to balance organization or project goals
- Practical guidance on using Benchmarks & Milestones: The Roadmap to Meeting Goals
- Understanding how subgoals and checklists add up to meet big goals
- A practical break down of "Why Tactics Aren't Goals" and clear examples to help you plan better

With the focus on Goals in mind, you'll see the word "goals" mentioned again and again throughout the book. Time and time again, what I see people struggle with the most in digital work, is defining their goals. Without that definition, people spend a lot of energy (and often money) on labor and movement that doesn't get them where they want to go. To make an excellent digital plan, you need to know your specific goals and focus on drafting a plan to meet them.

It's important not to have big lofty goals, but to be able to break them down into actionable steps and milestones. This section will give you the framework for the milestones and the sections of the book will help you work through the actionable steps. If you feel like you have a solid grasp on the function of goals in planning, go ahead and skip to structure.

Goals—Why you need them

Digital is part science and part art. The part most important to your actual plan is the science. Good digital is built around the science or technical side, great digital is both art and science, and mediocre digital work is often when you focus on only the science or art side. I've met and talked to plenty of people that have a digital, new media, or communications department that don't have clear and specific goals. Making videos, building websites, and sending some tweets are not goals, and they don't serve as a good plan. Digital tools are the means by which you and your organization will accomplish your goals.

During the 2012 cycle, we had three main goals for the digital department: raise money, win votes, and get more volunteers to fulfill the campaign's field mission. If we couldn't clearly tie an action to one of those three things, we did not do it. Goals acted as the starting point from which all of our actions were based. You will have moments with the luxury of creative time and other moments of pure execution within your goals and plan. A good digital plan and team are masters of goals and focus on them well to move progress forward.

Smart goals start with the pinnacle and work their way back into a plan. It should never go the other way. Our main campaign goal in 2012 started with getting Barack Obama re-elected. What that truly meant was moving a core group of voters in the battleground states and maintaining the electoral votes in the traditionally blue states. The digital team had the big-picture goals mentioned above—raise money, win votes, and get more volunteers to do the voter outreach. Each of these main goals were broken down into sub-goals and department-specific goals. What actions would work towards these goals as a web-developer, graphic designer, ad buyer, or videographer?

Unless each staffer of your digital team knows what the specific goals of the organization are and how they relate to their role, it is pretty easy to head down rabbit holes where people do cool things but don't meet the greater campaign goals. A plan with clearly defined goals not only keeps your team on track, it also helps with tough conversations around performance evaluations. Finding yourself in the scenario where people are working on projects that aren't mission critical while critical pieces go unattended, can be avoided when everyone knows the mission, its goals, and their part in it.

All too often, many organizers find themselves in one of two places: either the organization's goals are clear but how to break them down into digital roles is not, or the digital and the art of communication roles are defined, but might actually be missing the mark on the mission-critical goals. The questions below are to help you avoid the above scenarios, and I recommend you don't do anything until you can clearly answer them.

Goals: What is the goal of this organization or project?

This should be one simple goal like electing Barack Obama, raising awareness about an issue, or producing a film.

WHAT ARE THE SUBGOALS OF THE ORGANIZATION?

For example, top-level goal of electing Barack Obama would have these sub-goals:
- Getting to 270 electoral votes by winning in X number of states
- Raising enough money to do that.
- Persuade and turn out enough votes.
- Organize enough volunteers and staff to do that.

RAISING AWARENESS ABOUT *X* ISSUE.

- Have legislation introduced in *X* state by the end of the year.
- Raise the online conversation by *X* percentage.
- Have the issue mentioned in the media *X* number of times by the end of the year.

Now that you know the big overarching goals, you have to decide what the goals of your digital program will be. Section by section, we'll be dissecting the nuanced questions you should be asking for each of the components of your plan. We will start with the big goals that drive decision making. Ideally, you will have no more than three to five big goals. Your specific teams will undoubtedly have more. Here are some examples of what this could mean.

The 2012 campaign digital team had three primary goals:

Raise money, win votes, and get more volunteers to fulfill the campaign's field mission.

Each department and project had its own goals. How the video team would approach each of these goals would look pretty different from how the Digital Ads team would approach the same goals. In the video department, individuals were tasked with creating videos that intertwined persuasion around issues with a personal story. The goals there would be around tailoring content to intended segments of voters and getting those voters to view the video. While the Ads team would take many nuanced approaches, they might be looking at placing said video content for persuasion or creating entirely different distilled graphic placement strategy also to win votes.

Battleground states had their own plans with goals. Here we are getting down to the brass tacks. Each state would know their universe of likely voters to register. That would, to some degree, change the goals on how many voters they needed to focus on for new voter GOTV (Get Out The Vote), versus likely voters, versus those still in the persuadable category. Along with this, they needed to have specific goals for the kind of earned media they think will help with both GOTV and persuasion. But none of the GOTV is going to happen unless they know how many contacts each volunteer makes per shift and how many staff plus volunteers it will take to reach the voters needed.

That state's digital team had a section of that plan. The state team would then need to layer in how emails, tweets, web pages, and online organizing were needed to align support in reaching those goals. Things like recruiting new volunteers, and building for events to meet the capacity goals. As well as things like direct asks to register to vote and trainings for how volunteers could use online tools to register others to vote.

That team had its own set of goals to meet those goals. This is where the team would breakdown volume and kinds of emails to meet those goals. Calendars of content around deadlines and events.

Each member of that team should have their own goals. Individuals would have clear (well campaigns are chaotic, so mostly clear) delineation of what pieces they were responsible for. Who is capturing live content? Who is drafting which email or blog? Who is running which training? Individual goals should be spelled out for the individuals.

If you're thinking that's a lot of goals, you're right! But it's essential to make sure every labor hour is directed at what is needed to win an election or move an issue. Let's say you're creating the digital plan for an issue-driven organization. Your digital goals could look something like this:

ISSUE ORGANIZATION DIGITAL TEAM:

- Tell the story of the Issue.
- Engage and build the supporter base.
- Drive action to move the issue.

Why isn't Tweeting or building a website part of the one of these goals? That's because those things are tactics and tools for meeting goals. You might see goals like post tweets or create X number of videos in a more detailed section of a plan, but it shouldn't be the main vision of a department. Knowing the difference between goals and tools or tactics is critical because completing a tactic might feel like a positive step forward, but if it doesn't change a broader goal, you haven't moved the mission.

Benchmarks & Milestones: The Roadmap to Meeting Goals

Identifying the main goal is the first step. One of the biggest failures in planning I've seen is people working in digital, nonprofit, or campaign operations without clear benchmarks or milestones. I often use the benchmarks and milestones interchangeably. Think of them as guideposts or markers on your way to meeting the big goals.

Lack of benchmarks or milestones leads to confusion, lack of accountability, and often failure. You need these guideposts to know if you are on or off track and why. Teams that use benchmarks and milestones have less confusion over where they are headed. Good benchmarks that are checked in on allow a team to know if they are achieving the intended productivity and help to optimize the impact in the world they want.

I know it can be tough to develop goals and benchmarks for the first time. That is why this book will walk you through the questions to get you to the right goals, and I'll provide suggestions for benchmarks and milestones you can create and customize to your specific goals.

A Story About Good and Bad Benchmarks and Milestones

During a planning session in spring of 2012, I sat down with a new Digital Director in a battleground state. They were very talented in video production and field organizing, but new to social media and digital plan writing. We had gotten into the piece of his plan where we were talking about Twitter growth. We already knew that if we grew our account and engaged local voters, we could expand the online discussion, recruit more volunteers, and potentially persuade more voters. The plan had a goal of around 3,000 new followers for the quarter. I asked where the number came from and what the benchmarks were.

The number was simply what had happened in prior quarter, and they hadn't thought about benchmarks at all. The next draft of the plan included the 3,000 followers very nicely and evenly broken down by month. That may have made me cringe even more. It did not take external factors into account, and it did not reflect any ambition for the program. It appeared as if programmatically, there wasn't anything that was going to impact the growth goal. Every organization has something that will make an impact, and numbers rarely run a flat line. Whether it is press, or running an ad, a proactive campaign has certain events or circumstances that impact the numbers. Even the smallest environmental nonprofit sees a surge on Earth Day and can be the local go-to for that day. Others run large ad campaigns that put their brand and online presence into the minds of consumers. Good plans should reflect and account for these impacts.

I told him to make the number aspirational but realistic. What if we made the number 7,000? They said great and made 7,000 the number. I asked him how he'd get there. That's where a qualitative plan and quantitative plan met to create real benchmarks. Would it be a gradual ramp up? Would it have growth points and plateaus? The benchmarks should lay in clear goals, and the milestones were the markers of when those goals will be met or significant events and actions impacting the project. That director has since gone on to be a Netroots speaker themselves.

Benchmarks allow you to do two things.

First, they help you evaluate, allocate, and prioritize resources. Second, they allow you to shift goals. If you've met 100% of the quarterly goal after a month, what do you do? Do you merely shift your end quarterly goal higher? Do you reallocate human capital and resources to another project? Or do you double down and add resources because that project is yielding good returns? There may not be a clear right answer, and there are many next moves. The only thing you can't do is just ignore the benchmark.

Benchmarks can sound abstract. Here is some guidance on ways to think about benchmarks and as we go through chapters, you'll get a stronger perspective on how to set benchmarks for your goals.

Percent to goal benchmark—It's a numerical breakdown of where you need to be at the end of the project. These work well when everyone who needs to read the plan knows the end goals. These are also helpful when you need to move in small increments. For example, while working with a really diverse range of Facebook pages, at one point my team collectively decided that 3-5% growth over the quarter is what we wanted. But for some accounts, that meant only acquiring a few hundred fans, while for others, it meant thousands. Using the % made it easier for everyone to be on the same page on what sustainable growth looked like.

Raw number benchmark—This type of benchmark is similar to percent to goal, but shows the raw number instead of percent. Some numbers are just visually better and can feel more impactful when going over the raw numbers. While plotting out a map for what we expected for online voter registration in Nevada, we had an end goal of 10,000. But this wasn't going to be linear growth. The numbers were going to jump wildly depending on ad buys, election cycle timing, and major events we were creating. Understanding that our benchmarks would move in very steep spikes and jumps, as opposed to an inaccurate linear graph, clarified our path to achieving our goal.

The milestone—Some goals aren't numerical, and that's when you need the milestone. This could be finalizing a contract with a vendor. Things like securing materials needed for a project. This could be a sub-piece of the project being finished, like the script for a video, a particular piece of a website, or a proposal for that. It's hard to have a percent to goal benchmark on hiring someone or having a contract. Use a milestone instead.

ANOTHER LOOK AT THE IMPOSSIBLE GOALS

While working with the Democratic National Committee, I had the pleasure of working on a team led by Natalie Foster and Josh Peck. They had the entire New Media team build one large project plan with goals and benchmarks. Most of the team knew their goals and the benchmarks. We would gather once a month to talk about our teams' goals, percent to goal, and the reasons behind the current status. With aspirational planning, if we make it to 100% to goal on 80-90% of our projects, we had really achieved something. Why not 100% you ask? We were relying on aspirational goals raising the bar for everything we were doing. They had a solid grasp of what we needed to achieve to move the mission forward, and getting to the 80-90% marks would mean we hit baseline success. But the plan was about stretching goals, and that meant planning for the aspirational 100%. With plans in motion to hit this new 100%, we would stretch ourselves and have a better understanding for what is possible.

Though this type of planning worked for us, I don't think this style of planning works everywhere. You would need top-level buy-in on the reasons for charting an aspirational course that may be out of reach. That level of agreement would require consideration around which goals fall into the achievable category and which fall under aspirational. If you need to build trust in your department, I would NOT recommend this kind of planning but actually the opposite. I would shoot for a plan where you exceed 80% of your goals and meet 100%.

Goals: Know Thy Goals and Know Thy Plan

I've watched plenty of people write plans and never internalize the plan or use it as their actual guideposts. Don't get trapped in the idea you are writing the plan for someone else. Sure! It may be needed for your supervisor or a board, but at the end of the day, it's for you or your program.

What I've seen from the most successful organizations, is tiers of plans clearly outlined with the top level goals for the entire organization. Top level plans shouldn't be digging into all of the rich details needed to execute the tiers below departments, teams, and individuals. Think of that as a plan that is a wide-lens vision of the work for three, six, or 12 months. Something that could easily be read by a board or group of funders. Deeper dives for departments and teams can include more nuanced goals. Then flesh out plans for individuals with goals that clearly build the work of the department or team plan. Those individual team members' plans should be really in the weeds and have many microbenchmarks for them and their projects.

Know what goes behind the benchmarks and final goals. People will ask, or at least they should. If you are the person, who should be asking then do. If the plan writer does not have concrete ideas, goals, and benchmarks behind the plan, then you're in trouble. This is a major goal of the book, equipping everyone at each stage of plan making to ask the right questions to have clear answers and build a winning plan from there!

Why Tactics Aren't Goals

Goals and tactics are two very different things.

> *Goals are the outcomes that you want to achieve. Tactics are the actions to get to those goals.*

Consistently, I see people confuse digital tactics with goals. Here is an example of a tactic misplaced as a goal that I often see around the use of video: Our goal is to make a video.

Your goal could be to raise awareness or get people to join a thing or to donate. But video is the tactical end to either of those goals. The question is, if one of those is the goal, does a video reach that goal for you? Is it part of a broader strategy to reach that goal?

We'll break this down in each section, but more often than not, the broad goal should not be a tactical thing, but an impact that is (ideally) measurable.

Summary

Goals are the first, and very well, most important step to develop your digital strategy. Start with a clear goal, and work backward into your plan using benchmarks and milestones. Benchmarks will help you to evaluate, allocate, and prioritize resources, as well as shift goals. MIlestones are non-numerical, achievable steps towards your goal. Remember that goals and tactics are very different, so remember to focus on your goals, and use tactics to get there.

Stories and Studies

Presented by Alexandra Woodard.

The Case for Investing in Relationships

ALEXANDRA WOODARD // Digital Organizing Director, *Organizing for Action* // @alex_woodward

As an industry, we have become incredibly efficient at mobilizing our lists. While it's not easy, we have it down to a formula, with room for a little mystery and magic and a lot of testing—we know, for the most part, what is likely to drive people to take action and what isn't. It's this skill that helped to turn people out over the last ten years and especially during this new administration, and it's a testament to the brainpower and creativity in the progressive movement.

It's with this optimism that I urge my fellow digital progressives to tackle a blind spot that has large-scale implications. While we've gotten a lot right, focusing on our current reality as strictly a political problem is as though we're debating how best to fix a house's kitchen when the whole foundation is being eaten away. Sure, the kitchen is central, but no one's cooking anything when the house caves in.

Mobilizing people to take action is not a social movement, it's putting out a [very important] dumpster fire. And given the Trump administration's track record of attacking every shred of progress and putting lives on the line, it's easy to grow fatigued—unless we make strategic choices about how we call on supporters to take action, they'll become even more cynical than before.

It comes down to this: Mobilizing is not a synonym for organizing. Organizing is power building; it's creating and sustaining relationships between people so that they will show up for each other, even when the going gets tough. Mobilizing is strategically activating that power at key moments. The two are distinct but interdependent, and they must both be invested in.

Digital is no different. Digital tools, simply put, allow us to execute both at scale—digital organizing by creating a sense of community, digital mobilizing by leveraging that community to call for change.

This is what we know intuitively, right? In order to have a tight crew that can bring the heat, you have to build and maintain relationships, a sense of belonging, and identity.

But aside from language choices, we're still in the baby stages of exploring how to do that online in a sustained, programmatic way.

Perhaps the problem is that we're making the assumption that people already have community, and all we have to do is tell them how to influence it. But overwhelmingly, social science research across disciplines concludes that is less and less true, and we'd be foolish to think that we can fix it solely by "doing politics better." In other words, the cohesion of our communities is at risk, and that affects our ability to influence decision-makers.

My stepfather's story is one example of what that can look like. He's a refugee from Lithuania, born at the beginning of the Soviet Union's takeover. The invaders were smart; they asked Lithuanians to give what seemed like benign information about the comings and goings of their neighbors and coworkers, and would then deduce who was likely to be a troublemaker. My step-grandfather, a chemist, was highly educated and a particular target. He refused to comply, and so they came after him. He escaped out of the back window of his office building, ran home to grab the family, and fled. Lithuania remained under Soviet control for nearly 50 years.

The Soviets had found a way to successfully destroy the connections between people. Even family members came to distrust one another. How do you form collective action to resist if you don't have a collective?

That was then—and maybe also now. A similar kind of social isolation is happening in ways that we're passively endorsing and even facilitating, and it's affecting—and will continue to affect—the politicians we elect, the way we're able to organize groups, and just how sustainable any social movement is.

This is not sudden, but it's becoming urgent. We've been cocooning since the 1970s, moving further and further away from participation in voluntary activities that bind communities together. This includes everything from member associations like the PTA, unions, religious organizations, free sports clubs, and yes, politics. Some of this shift is generational; older Americans are more communally oriented, whether it's because they had to come together during a world war or civil rights movements, or because the suburbs weren't totally a thing yet. Certainly, pressures on time and money influence the degree to which people participate in voluntary activities, but according to the data, not as much as we might expect. Technology, on the other hand—the car, television, air conditioner, and now, the smartphone—has a significant impact in pulling us further apart from one another and into the privacy of our own homes, redefining how we create community. The advent of anywhere, anytime access to the internet has only expedited the trend. In June 2016, American adults spent on average 10 hours and 39 minutes interacting with screens—that's time not spent in community with others that you could, say, show up to your rep's office with.

I'm highly critical of arguments that make hyperbole out of technology. Smartphones are just tools; would you say a hammer is causing the disintegration of our communities? A hunk of lithium and silicon isn't, either.

But what researchers are bringing up is an important point: How we're using them could be. Since the release of the iPhone in 2007, rates of depression and suicide—especially among teens—have spiked, and the data confirm that it's tied to loneliness. We may be more connected to more people than ever before, but it's affecting how we relate to ourselves and others. One generational study finds that driver's licenses have declined in demand among teens—they feel less necessary when interaction can take place via social media. Our use of technology is a convenient distraction from activities that force us to interact with people of differing opinions or behavior, as uncomfortable as those interactions may be, and find a way to be compassionate.

In fact, the American Psychological Association released a study in August 2017 that suggests that "social isolation, loneliness could be greater threat to public health than obesity," and even as recently as October 2017, former Surgeon General Vivek Murthy has sounded the alarm.

So, as far as politics are concerned, it's not necessarily a question of whether our messages are powerful enough, people aren't convinced enough, or the testing isn't smart enough—even though those are all important. If we're more lonely and less enmeshed in the lives of those in our immediate proximity, we become aliens to each other, making diversity and conversation a scary thing—and border walls and guns a matter of safety and identity. We lose our very strength: Our togetherness.

Yet a 24-hour inventory of one's email inbox can show pretty definitively that advocacy campaigns' priority is mobilization, not relationship formation. An extreme example of this is the hotly-debated emergency emails with subject lines like "URGENT: Status pending" or "I'm begging you, Alexandra." Sure, they may be effective at getting people to respond with a signature or a dollar, but they often burn trust, and they certainly don't encourage a sense of community. Sending out personal stories in mass emails doesn't heal all wrongs, either—sure, they help personalize the issue, but are we actually using them to build a sense of community?

We already know we can use digital tools to mobilize people—but we need to help feed the soul of our movement by examining how well we're bringing people together. This work isn't just for field staff—we have an opportunity, right now, to change the playing field by using the tools at our disposal to build real community so that we're in a stronger position to take action when we need them to.

I realize this is hard. But as we say at OFA, we've never been here for the easy fights. If you have a way to quantify social capital development via email campaigns, I want your number.

Fortunately, we have highly regarded research to draw from that can help us invest in both our organizing and mobilizing tactics online. I invite collaboration; please contact me at awoodward@ofa.us.

STRUCTURE

The art of writing any good plan is knowing your audience. Often in digital, we use the term audience for the receivers of content and your plan is no different. You will need to make some decisions on who the reader is and how far in the weeds they need information. This will change what the presentational structure will look like because you need a plan that strikes the right balance of information and functionality.

How to use this chapter

Non-Digital Leadership or Management: This chapter is helpful for you to understand how structuring a digital plan might look different.

Digital/Tech Staffers: This chapter is designed for you to better understand that you're not alone in your challenges, practical advice for those growing in their roles as strategists, and ways to plan better.

New Staff/Activists: This chapter will help you understand how you might build a plan. It may be more than is needed for your projects now, but helpful as you grow in this space.

KEY TAKEAWAYS AND ELEMENTS:
- Ways to structure a draft of a digital plan
- Possible problems you might run into with plan drafting

- Some real barriers that those who are more artistically or analytically driven have had with planning
- Real examples on how to deliver a plan that meets your needs on the project in front of you. Every project is different

Hopefully, you know who your audience is, at least in broad terms. Your audience could be your board, an executive or department director, funder, or staff. You should know what the expectations are of the audience you are delivering to. Are they expecting top lines and bullets, long, insightful paragraphs, or some combination of the two? It's your job as the plan writer to be sure you know this information. If you just write a plan and send it off without knowing the expectations of your audience, there is a solid chance you should expect a serious redraft.

Here are a few key questions you should ask about a draft you need to deliver to someone else.

- Is there a maximum or minimum length expected?
- Is there a preferred template the final plan should fit?
- Is the expectation for it to be about top lines and finished products?
- How can you show benchmarks and milestones?
- How can you illustrate the plan without showing all the details?
- How in the weeds do you need to, go (i.e., digital wonk or no wonk)?

Structure: Drafting

Once you have some answers, you should start drafting. The real key is just starting and not worrying too much about the end structure. You will probably find one or both of these to be true:

- The final delivery of the plan to an audience not directly executing the work is not likely to be detailed enough to efficiently run a project or program day-to-day.
- The structure of the plan might not fit how your brain works.

Start by writing the plan you need to run your program or project. Never constrain what you need to meet goals to a product that needs to be delivered to stakeholders who are not executors. If you only need to deliver a two-page plan, but you know your program needs a 20-page in-depth guide with micro-benchmarks to the day, then write that plan.

Take that 20-page plan, distill it for delivery and use it personally for you and your team to achieve everything you said you'd do. That distilled plan will guide you to success.

Possible Problems with Drafting

An artist, a data scientist, and a web developer walk into a bar... One draws or writes about it. One analyzes it. One considers the user experience of it.

The modern digital team in many organizations is a beautiful mixture of people with very, very different disciplines. Quite literally, your brains work differently.

ARTIST MEETS DRAFTING

You might be part of a digital team or project because you are a little more creative than many members of your staff. But your brain doesn't see the world the same way your friend in operations does. Maybe you find yourself staring at the template you've been given, and it just doesn't work for what you need to do. My advice is don't write it that way. I've run into this same problem myself. I've looked at the template and tried to start writing in someone else's structure, and it just doesn't work.

Two days later, I walked into a room with a whiteboard and started mapping one piece of my internal plan on a whiteboard. I knew one of the end goals I needed to get to, and I had a calendar of events that led to that goal. But my mind needed the big visual to see the steps and fill in the gaps. Once I felt good about what was on the board, I put it to paper (a word document). I subsequently worked through other pieces and drafted the plan in the structure I am most comfortable with (which is bullets, top lines, and a lot of benchmarks connected to events and days). I first mapped the plan I needed and then distilled it into what was needed from me. There was one extra addendum that didn't fit the exact template I was given, but I explained how it was helpful and was thanked for being thoughtful about the process.

THE ANALYTIC MEETS DRAFTING

On the flip side, you might be a numbers-driven person. Everything about benchmarking and milestones that are numerical might be ideal for you, and it's the question of how to quantify the time for the creative side that is the mental block. We'll dig into that a bit more in the sections related to creative processes like writing, design, and video because it takes grounding in the art to make that possible.

Structure: Delivery

If you just need to deliver a straightforward two-page document, then this might be easy enough. Chances are though, you'll need to read through the plan with leadership peers, your supervisor, and at the very least, with the team you're working with. This is the part that goes back to internalizing your plan. If you are working on a large plan where you have other teams writing their piece, you'll want to spend some time with them knowing more deeply what goes into their plan.

If you need to formally present your plan in front a large group, say with a presentation, here are a few tips to make sure you get the buy-in you need and deserve.

TIP #1 ON DELIVERY: BE SLEEK, DATA-DRIVEN, AND EFFICIENT.

I think of modern digital as these three things. Sleek design builds branding and can drive action. If design lives within your department, then your presentation should be the best looking one on the screen that day.

Data is why digital is real. We have evolved beyond the early days of social media and motives such as, "It's about being social," and "We do it because it gives our brand personality." Nowadays, we either have, or are building, data to make better decisions on quality of impact. You have data on the impact of tools, channels, and investments your team is making and can produce. Share that data, be real with that data. (Also, if you read this book and then present a plan and use the term viral, I will haunt you. I promise my digital ghost will haunt you).

Efficiency: The presentation should be as efficient as possible because part of what the world is looking for from digital tools and technology is efficiency. The final reason people are making these investments in digital is the efficiency it adds to all kinds of engagement and messaging. Digital accomplishes things like building new conversation channels with supporters and consumers because it takes traditional paid advertising like commercials and gives it more depth online, with tracking ability, and a wider reach across social media.

TIP #2 ON DELIVERY: DIFFERENT ISN'T ALWAYS BETTER.

The best example of this that I've witnessed was the Prezi explosion of 2012. A number of people wanted to present something using Prezi but didn't take the time to really understand Prezi. I don't mean the how to zoom and pan but why to zoom and pan. They looked like a Powerpoint had vomited on a Prezi and zoomed around that mess.

I love both traditional slide programs like Powerpoint and Prezi, but they are different and should each be treated with an artistic eye. Most importantly, just adding new flashy things to your presentation doesn't make it better. Same goes for just making the presentation over-stylized, having too many animations (I've been guilty of that), or using additions that may or may not perform 100% every time.

TIP #3 ON DELIVERY: BE VISUAL.

If you are talking about three million viewers, then you should show a proper representation of three million viewers. Less text is always, always better. If you're talking about Twitter, it could look like a Twitter timeline or Facebook page, Tumblr, SnapChat, Pinterest, or other familiar site. If you are influencing 10,000 voters, show a voter being influenced and the tools that will do it, and use your voice to talk about that. Don't write that all on the board. To put these tips into practice, here are is a checklist to bring it home.

> The plan presentation checklist:
> - Have I walked through it several times?
> - Did a second or third eye copy edit my work?
> - Does it work offline if needed?
> - Do I know the material?
> - Will it play on the device I am using?
> - Do I need handouts?

Summary

Drafting a plan means creating a structure catered to both you and your specific audience. The best way to deliver digital content is to be sleek, data-driven and efficient. Make your content more engaging by adding visuals, and remember that different isn't always better. Know your audience, and keep it simple.

Stories and Studies

Presented by Jay Carmona.

Digital Tracking and Engagement

JAY CARMONA // Founder, Sematonic Strategies // @jaycarmona

Have you ever gotten conflicting messages at work? One manager telling you to do one thing one way, and another telling you to do it another way entirely?

In a role as leader of a digital department at an advocacy organization running several campaigns, I started to notice that I got this sick feeling in the pit of my stomach as I opened up the files for new campaign plans. Sometimes, the plans would be minor in terms of digital work, occasionally even helpful to narrow my scope of work and provide strategic insight. Too often though, the campaign plan would show me what I dreaded: a long list of digital "metrics" for tasks I was to perform in advance. The main strategy for myself and the digital department as part of these plans was often to "get eyes on it." I dreaded the phrase, "get the word out" in grant applications and campaign plans alike. These plans often gave me additional objectives to meet, and as a nearly equally bad alternative, I would get the job of coming up with my own objectives and metrics (after the plan was mostly approved) to reflect success on a plan for this digital strategy of "getting the word out." I would often spend long periods of time with these campaign plans, peppering them with comments, questions, or potential edits. I also found myself throwing out my own plan for the digital department in favor of tracking all of the disparate metrics for multiple campaigns. All the same, due to my own duties and also at the level I was at in the organization, I could not participate in multiple campaign and departmental planning processes as well as a process for my own department. I found myself torn between many campaign objectives for several different, ineffective, digital strategies, at the expense of the departmental planning that I had done, which included longer-term tool improvement, web development, and staff mentorship and training. Longer-term, digital infrastructural projects that would benefit all campaigns and the organization had to be lowest in priority.

The organization had a theory of change, but I've noticed that some theories of change can be open to a startlingly large number of interpretations in regards to digital work.

Let me put it this way: there are thousands of digital tools, platforms, and gimmicks out there, and they often are being pitched to my inbox at fastball speed. I know firsthand that digital staff are under a lot of pressure. Added to that is pressure to "go viral" as a success strategy (it's not a success strategy), to create content, write, and to administer increasingly complex digital systems. In this environment, chasing any metric without knowing why you're doing it, let alone differing metrics for multiple campaigns, is an extremely difficult task. It is also incredibly time-consuming.

I needed a way to open conversations at the organization about digital engagement, as well as digital planning and strategy. I needed a way to illustrate the issues from the perspective of digital, where the rubber was hitting the road, and the differing takes on my department's work were coming into starker conflict. I took this as an opportunity to build and visualize an organization-wide supporter engagement journey, a document showing how our supporters build a relationship with our organization's digital and organizing systems, starting from the first piece of content they saw and moving to a much deeper level of engagement (or trust or initiative) with the organization. This document could also illustrate our organizational strategy across departments and campaigns for planning purposes. It could also illustrate where we were trying to do too much, or not enough. Besides the end product being helpful, the conversations with campaign and department heads in the context of building and refining that journey would be constructive could build buy-in for a more unified digital strategy and could help me illustrate where issues were happening. It was clear from my position that supporters were being asked to do too many versions of the same action (usually, signing a petition), without being provided enough opportunities for taking action beyond that, to grow their relationship to the organization. I needed a way to illustrate the trends that I was seeing to colleagues who had varying understanding of digital tools and strategy.

As I started to have conversations with department heads and campaigning leads at my organization about where they were taking supporters, it became clearer that we had many differing takes on where we were trying to take supporters, and how we were going to get them there. I was able to show, using simple flowchart diagrams, our engagement infrastructure.

Our Development department, for example, already had a ladder of engagement, but for their purposes, and understandably, the highest-level supporter on their cycle was a donor. Most campaigning or organizing efforts would probably look different if all departments were only trying to turn every supporter into a donor. We had to expand our view of what our highest-level supporter would be doing so that we could discuss our process for getting them there. Different campaign leads also had different takes on how supporters would work with one another. One campaign was starting to form in-person, local campaigning groups while others were aimed at changing the behavior of targets via public pressure. There were differing opinions on what supporters on social media could do beyond signing a petition or sending a letter if anything at all.

Creating an organization-wide engagement cycle wasn't just about filling in the right template. The central conversation was this: What is the most organized, skilled up, committed supporter going to be doing, right before we win? It's probably not just sharing content; it's not even just producing content. Are they leading a group? Are they recruiting others to join a group or campaign? Meeting with targets? Running a canvass? My advice is this: Figure out what your most-organized supporters need to be doing, figure out where the least organized supporters are coming in (probably seeing a piece of your content on social media through a friend) and fill in the middle steps to get people from start to finish. That will tell your digital staff why they are doing something, and it will help align the different components of your digital strategy, all the way down to content.

After getting a picture of the different engagement journeys of our departments and campaigns, and representing those via a visual map, I was able to show how the organizational strategy could be stronger: we were overemphasizing a multitude of low-level digital actions in our work, and providing little or no opportunities beyond donating for supporters. The numbers from our CRM backed that up as well, though we found it was also more difficult to track our digital to offline conversions—so there was a certain margin of error with the metrics there, but it was clear that 70-90% of our supporters were stuck in a cycle of petition-signing. Not only were the holes in the diagram visual to all, I could tell a corresponding narrative of a user's journey from a first-person standpoint. "I've been a supporter for two years, I've signed 10 petitions, I've written five letters, I've attended two webinars, I want to do more, what do I do next?" Through individual conversations, I also realized that some staff were not able to imagine what supporters could do beyond signing petitions, or how to engage them at deeper levels with our work, and they couldn't plan what they hadn't yet imagined. This basic failure of digital "imagination" was causing us to repeat and cement our issues into our planning processes.

At the end of the process of developing the engagement cycle, many more staffers were able to more clearly articulate all the steps on our supporter engagement journey, and why they were each important, but the issues with campaign and strategic problems still remained. In order to try to unify strategies, I proposed that supporters should be transitioned between campaigns that brought them into the level of signing and sharing petitions, and campaigns that sought to give higher level asks, like action organizing, participating in offline groups, and creating content for the organization, and with the engagement cycle I was able to illustrate why that step was needed, and why campaigns with in-person opportunities were critical. These conversations enabled some of the campaigns to bring my department into planning processes earlier, in order to develop digital objectives that matched directly with their campaigning objectives from the beginning in planning, as Brad suggests in this book.

The engagement cycle planning helped staffers, and myself, to imagine how our digital and organizing materials built a relationship with supporters over time, and how each department and campaign at the organization participates in this process together. The truth is, digital departments can be a lot of things to different people. We can be a content factory, website and CMS technicians, organizers, campaigners, fundraisers, communications hubs, and a host of other things. Given all of these demands, digital departments need to know why we are asking supporters to take an action, and also what action supporters will be asked to take next, or the danger of overwhelm, competing priorities, and stories that lack coherence becomes far too high.

 **STAFF**

So you've got the skeleton of a plan and realize you don't have the staff needed to create it, or you are drafting a plan for a project or department that doesn't even exist yet. It's on you to figure out who you need. As you contemplate this task feeling slightly overwhelmed with stress, you should know you're not alone. Outside of a relatively small but growing group of people, very few people have run a large digital program or enough holistic digital programs to know exactly what they need. Every developer, designer, and social media expert is different. Part of plan writing is getting a sense of who you really need.

How to use this chapter

Non-Digital Leadership or Management: This chapter is helpful for you to understand staffing a department with really different skill sets.

Digital/Tech Staffers: Practical knowledge for you as you grow and start to manage your own team.

New Staff/Activists: Worth a look if you are joining a new team.

KEY TAKEAWAYS AND ELEMENTS:
- Thoughts on internal development vs. hiring outside skilled talent
- Quick thoughts on team culture

Clarifying who you need comes in the form of quality expectation and knowing exactly what it is you are trying to do. I've watched a video team of one-and-half full-time people create 12 videos in eight weeks, and a team of six create four videos in the same number of weeks, but they were producing different videos with different goals. The same could easily be said for social media: I've watched one good person really develop one really engaging twitter account, and one good person develop four less engaging accounts. Both cases were strategically correct uses of time, given different goals.

Here are some of the initial questions that should be asked:
- What are the biggest programmatic goals we need to achieve?
- What kind of budget do we have?
- Do we need people that can perform multiple tasks such as video planning (producing), shooting, and editing or people who are focused on just one task like graphic design or shooting?
- Do we need several good generalists (basic HTML coding, writing, some video editing)?
- At what point do we need managers of people?

INSIDERS VS. SPECIALIZED SKILLS

This might be a real issue you'll run up against especially if you're in a nonprofit that likes to hire from inside the same organization or field. But if you are running a team inside any institution, you should consider it. Will you hire someone who is loyal to the organization and wants to grow as part of the team, or will you bring in someone from outside? This might sound abstract but should be well considered. I've watched both go well and poorly. Especially if you are an organization with a really specific culture and mission. Here is an example to consider.

We were hiring state digital directors for the 2012 campaign. We had solid leads of people from inside and outside the organization. There were two candidates in two different states. Both had worked in the field working directly with volunteers, so they understood the core mission of the organization at the state level.

Candidate one had a great background with us and had also been managing the state's social networks for that given state. They didn't have much digital knowledge beyond that. They had a clear aptitude and vision to learn more. In the end, they built one of the best digital programs in one of the most critical battlegrounds. They had the aptitude to plan, write, grow, ask the questions they didn't know, and bring on the people needed to fill gaps.

Candidate two had the field background but also worked in video production. Video is a difficult skill. They knew they lacked the other components like social media strategy, but were eager to learn. They, unfortunately, had to change roles after two months. It just wasn't the right fit and left us with a gaping hole.

To be honest, there is not a magic solution to change candidate two into candidate one. Candidate two was later replaced by someone from outside the organization because the decision was made we didn't have the time to develop someone from the inside. They quickly understood the culture and applied their knowledge to that culture and program.

One of the biggest factors in choosing whether or not to work from the inside vs. outside is time. Do you have the time to develop someone? Do you believe they'll stay on longer if you do? If you have a small project or limited window, I would—more often than not—hire skills from outside rather than try to develop it from the inside.

AN IMPORTANT NOTE ON CULTURE

When building a team, you need to decide what is most important for your team culture. I've met some really skilled people who just didn't gel with their team. This actually killed the overall production of a team. It's up to you to set the tone and hire the people that fit that team or, in time, cut the folks that don't fit.

If you are going to build a team of people who just show up and execute and clock out when their project is done, that's fine, but make sure everyone you hire fits that team. The same is to be said if you are trying to build a close-knit team. Don't hire that person who wants to sit in a dark room and edit, code, or write and never talk if collaboration is important to their role and team. If you feel the need to hire someone who might not be a perfect cultural fit, talk to them about it. Make sure you are deliberate and give them the reasons why it might be difficult. I promise you, both you and the hire will be happier either way. The bad scenario is hiring someone with the skills who underperforms because they dislike showing up to their environment. But a great scenario is one where everyone flourishes because you have built an intentional community in your department or project team.

Summary

Hiring and working with the right staff to reach your goals starts with clarity about the goal your working towards. Then consider whether you'd like to work with staff within your organization, or hire outside for specialized skills. Remember to consider the culture of your team, and be intentional about where and how you may work together.

Stories and Studies

Presented by Gabe Smalley, Chris Burley, and Aditi Juneja.

The Art of Saying "No"

GABE SMALLEY // Digital Campaigns Manager, *Rainforest Action Network* // http://bit.ly/2pElzJg

As digital campaigning becomes more mainstream, more of the folks that we work for are learning just enough about the space to think they're informed, and as such, to weigh in with decisions that aren't always the most strategic. Instead of immediately pushing back, especially against powerful campaigners or candidates, it's best to take a bad idea and start asking questions. If you can dig down to the actual measurable goals, you can recommend alternatives that are more strategic, have bigger impacts, or require fewer resources. As a last resort, if you hear a particularly bad idea that you can't think of a polite response to in the moment, offer to "bounce it off" another expert in the field while you think of a diplomatic way to present smarter alternatives.

Swing Outside Your Strike Zone

CHRIS BURLEY // Independent Consultant // @cburley

Remember 2008? The embarrassing number of times you played that Will.i.am. song? It was a memorable year—the year Sarah Palin taught me to really start worrying and plan to be nimble.

In summer 2008, the wildlife and environment-focused organization I worked with wasn't particularly interested in digital campaigning around the presidential election. Believing the best use of dollars would be to squarely focus on House and Senate campaigns, the organization planned to mainly sit out the 2008 presidential contest.

But sometimes organizations—like great baseball players—need to be flexible. They need to stretch themselves to make the most of an opportunity. They need to swing for the fences.

Only when GOP Senator John McCain selected former Alaska Governor—and known fan of gunning down wolves from helicopters—Sarah Palin as his pick for vice president, did the organization realize the role it might play in the election.

Many within the organization and the DC punditry class wondered if voters, and women especially, might not be energized by this "plain-spoken" western governor. Some in the organization worried that endorsing one political party's candidate over the other would alienate the organization's less political supporters, reducing its influence, support from members, and—ultimately—effectiveness.

On the other hand, the Obama-Biden ticket's policies were far more clearly aligned with the organization's vision for a better world. Sarah Palin only had a brief time in public office, but she had already distinguished herself as an ally of Big Oil and a supporter of extreme predator control. Also, SHE LIKED SHOOTING WOLVES FROM HELICOPTERS.

If the organization was to play a role in keeping an anti-environment extremist away from the White House, a decision had to be made. But becoming involved in the presidential election could be a tremendous political opportunity or a damaging miscalculation that would squander precious resources and political capital.

This group had clear protocols for rapid response. It had the staff and technical resources to achieve the organization's goals in taking on Palin. And it had the good sense to realistically plan the sort of campaign the moment demanded.

Key staff, consultants, and leadership were quickly assembled. Decisions were made. Action steps outlined. Assignments accepted. Expectations articulated.

In the end, an organization with absolutely no plans to participate in the 2008 election did exactly that, and they shifted course within a span of just hours.

As a result, the group was able to air one of the most influential political ads of the 2008 election. The spot aired in seven battleground states was covered extensively in the national political press, and helped establish a national narrative about how ridiculously unsuited Palin was to be vice president, let alone president, should the need arise.

The moral to the story? Sometimes you have to be prepared to swing outside the strike zone for the grand slam you didn't know you were looking for.

Self-care When It's Your Job to Be Plugged In

ADITI JUNEJA // Creator and Host, *Self Care Sundays* // www.aditijuneja.me

I first understood how self-care works in the context of digital strategy around the, now infamous, "covfefe" tweet. This typo by the President created a lot of speculation and mockery on social media. It was also completely irrelevant to the organization I was running at the time, Resistance Manual. When I checked in with Jess Talwar, our intern, who was managing rapid response on our social media, she brought it up. I gently reminded her that it was not relevant to our work. Still, she was intrigued by it. So, I tried a different approach—I told her that, even though it was her job to be plugged in, she doesn't have to be plugged into everything. In fact, I advised her that it is a good self-care practice to create mental boundaries around what she will and will not entertain online since she cannot completely disconnect.

Later that week, I discussed this anecdote with Beth Becker, a progressive digital strategist, on my podcast Self Care Sundays. She paused and told me that her staff member had also told her earlier that day not to engage in things over which she has no control. Since leaving Resistance Manual, I have managed social media for two different organizations and come to appreciate how challenging the advice that I gave Jess, and that Beth was given, is to follow. As a digital strategist, you are always looking to connect your organization's goals or brand to broader cultural moments. You are looking for the opportunity to hit just the right tone, in just the right way, so that your tweet or post goes viral. It can be hard not to engage.

Still, these boundaries over our mental real estate are deeply important given that we don't always have the luxury of disconnecting. During our episode, Beth shared with me how challenging the months after the 2016 election were for people who worked in digital strategy and social media. In the months since that interview with her, I have come to increasingly believe that when you can't turn it off, you have to be extremely disciplined about what you will or will not focus on. Additionally, I've come to realize that you have to be honest with yourself about what truly requires a rapid response.

The vast majority of content that my bosses have sent to me when I was working for organizations could wait a couple of hours to be shared. In fact, I sometimes got a higher engagement rate by waiting until the initial storm was over and sharing more thoughtful content. Most people aren't on social media all day. When they plug in and are trying to figure out what happened a few hours before, my "delayed" post was actually useful in helping people catch up. I realize this isn't possible for everyone, but for me, it has allowed me to take real breaks to go to a show or sleep without waking up in the middle of the night to check my phone. Doing things that you enjoy and resting are crucial parts of self-care.

In a similar vein, I think trusting the team that you're working with allows you to take those shorter breaks and even longer vacations. As a co-founder of an organization, I understand the fear of turning over your passwords to volunteers and completely disconnecting. As a person who ended last summer tired in the depths of my soul, I also know that it's really important. If you are fortunate enough to be able to take a vacation, you have to trust others enough to really take it. Even if it's just an hour at the gym a day (and ideally it's both daily breaks and longer ones), you need the time to reset and refocus. I can feel readers rolling their eyes at this point, thinking that rest is for mortals and not martyrs. However, on that podcast episode, Beth and I agreed that martyr would become an insult, not a badge of honor.

It is noble to sacrifice yourself for a cause, but it is likely more useful if you are alive and well to fight for it. None of us are in a position to respect our audiences if we're not taking the time to respect ourselves and our needs. As digital professionals, we need to find our moments of peace so that we can engage in ways that are compassionate and helpful, rather than getting caught up in what is often an angry cesspool. If we can do this, we can respect each other's differences in a way that allows us to build together and maybe even across differences. Given the inherent loneliness associated with being a digital professional, with large portions of us working remotely, I think we have a duty to make the online spaces where we are interacting with others pleasant ones.

We also need to find the time to do the things that feed our souls and replenish us. We need to find time to spend with the people who see us not as brands or messages, but as full people who exist in complicated and contradictory ways. We need friends who appreciate our small efforts to remain connected across time and space. We need to take care of our bodies and to step away from screens. During Season 1 of Self Care Sundays, I observed that most people became intentional about self-care after experiencing significant burnout. As a result, I have become a huge advocate of self-care as prevention to more extreme and dangerous exhaustion. I believe that technology, like anything else, has its positives and its negatives and we should treat it as such. It is only useful to the extent that it improves our lives. It is up to us, as digital professionals, to make sure that it does for ourselves so that we can help ensure that it does for others as well.

WEBSITE AND WEB DEVELOPMENT

Everyone needs a site these days, and for non-techies and techies alike, it can be a gargantuan project. Maintaining focus on your goals, and working to keep the project as simple and straightforward as possible will help streamline your website project.

How to use this chapter

Non-Digital Leadership or Management: A compelling read to help you understand the many layers of web development and where the challenges and costs exist. It will make you better equipped to ask the right questions and make sure your web developments succeeds.

Digital/Tech Staffers: Regardless of its role in the digital realm, web development is hard. Web development often means pulling together every tool in the toolbox and discipline needed from your team or contractors.

New Staff/Activists: This will help you understand why web development is hard and costly but can be tackled with a good plan.

KEY TAKEAWAYS AND ELEMENTS:
- Foundational understanding of websites and web development and when to tackle projects

- Practical examples of building new sites, building on existing work, or having to rebuild your organization's website
- Approaches to process, priorities, and long-term planning
- A clear set of steps for Project Planning for Web Development

The most significant beast of burden for digital teams and projects right now may very well be web development. Here are the three biggest hurdles I've seen and experienced over the years:

1. **Unrealistic scope of a project** in funding, timing, need, or ability.

2. **Designing web pages or tools for a small audience** that did not serve the core audience needed to meet larger goals.

3. **Bloat** including bells and whistles distracting from the core website actions you need people to take. Or just too many damn things on a page.

Each of these problems and hurdles occurs when the goals can't be well defined or put into a hierarchy.

We'll break this part of the book down into a few sections, which will help you figure out a plan. If you are starting a big new project, this might be the hardest goliath you'll encounter of any of the digital planning elements.

It is essential to start with asking yourself the question of whether or not to launch a new web development project and if that is the best way to meet your goals. Relative to that will be identifying the type of project you are tackling.

- A new organization or campaign
- A new project
- Rebuilding an existing site

From there you can dig into the processes of planning out your capacity and delve into the structural planning and timelines to make sure the sum of the work and effort adds up to meeting your goals.

Website and Web Development: To build or not to build? That should be the question.

If you are launching a new project or organization not connected to another entity, this question may be relatively straightforward.

But before you start any project, you need to know: what is your #1 goal? Can you break it down into the top three sub-goals working toward the long-term goals of the organization?

If you are starting from scratch and goal #1 is to build a website, then that seems pretty straightforward.

So let's pause here and split the question into three sections.

Start below for a new organization or campaign, if you are at square one with your project or campaign. Skip down to the section of Web Development called "New Project," if you have an existing website and you are working on a plan for a micro-site or approaching development for a specific future project. Lastly, if you have a website but need to revamp the entire thing, jump to the "Rebuilding an Existing Site" section.

Website and Web Development: For new organization or campaign

You just need a website. Sounds simple enough but you should answer the next few questions before you endeavor to build your website.

What needs to happen on the website on day one?

What needs to happen on the website at the 30-day, three-month, six-month marks?

Do you have the capacity to build this in-house or do you need to contract out?

The question on day one, day 30, three months, six months, and one year will dictate a lot of the planning and work that will need to go into the site.

The platform options will dictate which CMS (Content Management System) you use. A CMS

BRAINSTORM AND PLAN

These questions are key to getting started:

1. *What are your milestones?*
2. *What is your capacity?*

system is how you post and create website content like a basic page, blog post, or donate page. CMS examples include WordPress, Squarespace, Drupal, Wix, Tumblr, NationBuilder, and more. CRM (Customer Relationship Management) systems can be pretty basic, but for organizational and campaign work it can get more complicated. Some people think of their email client as their CRM. Examples include MailChimp, Constant Contact, and BlackBaud. When choosing the CRM that is right for you, you may want it integrated with some of your site speciality pages like petitions, donate pages, and sign-ups. In this case, you would need something like Blue State Digital, ActionKit, Action Network, Salsa, Convio from BlackBaud, NationBuilder, or Every-Action. But if you are doing deep volunteer management or connecting to a voter file, you will probably have to choose between EveryAction from NGPVAN or Nation-Builder. Your head might be spinning now. This is also a major question on how many database tools you'll need to connect. Please take some time and reference the Data and Analytics section.

You might be thinking, "Whoa we don't have time to decide what we want, we just need a page up next week!" That's okay too, as long as you know your day one, day 30, three months, six months, and 12-month goals. These milestones are important for you to prioritize how you'll manage the content and building of new pages and tools.

Here are a few examples that may be helpful for you to think through what you'll need at each stage, and how to start the most basic selection process.

The long run is simple—

Let's say you are doing a pretty simple informational campaign and that you'll just want to make basic info available and you aren't driving donations or petitions.

Day 1: Basic three-page site is live—About Org, About Campaign, Sign-Up
Day 30: Expanded materials like PDFs and other info
3 Month: Basic Updates
6 Month: Basic Updates
12 Month: Basic Updates

"Basic updates" this might look bland but it is a placeholder for information like new blogs, updating your basic information, or pages that exist. It is a recognition that you might not be expecting more development work but just content maintenance. Even if it is a robust series of blogs that should appear in a content calendar not a website production plan.

If this looks like what you need then keep it simple and go with something like WordPress or Squarespace. Stylize a good template and focus on the other work.

Let's say your goals are a little more complicated, and you need donate and event pages. Question here is, do you need them on day one, day 30, or three months in?

It's important to make clear decisions on what you need for day one of the website launch because two different projects could look like the following:

SCENARIO #1

Day 1: Basic three-page site is live—About Org, About Campaign, Sign-Up

Day 30: Donate page live, Blog Live, Events pages live

3 Month: News Releases Live

6 Month: Updates to the homepage, About

12 Month: Basic updates continue

SCENARIO #2

Day 1: More robust site is live; About Org, About Campaign, Sign-Up, Donate page live, Blog live, Events pages live, News Releases Live,

Day 30: Updates to homepage; Capacity to update all functions continue

3 Month: Basic updates continue

6 Month: Basic updates continue

12 Month: Basic updates continue

These two scenarios might look pretty similar, but the outcomes can be drastically different. Consistently in the past, people new to web development often want Scenario #2 because they believe it is best to have everything all at once. That means done and ready. But websites are rarely done. Everyone who knows anything about website development will tell you it's about ongoing updates and iterations.

To make Scenario #2 a reality, the project planner might say, "We'll just add capacity or start earlier." But this doesn't account for focus and testing. You aren't just gaining time in what has to be produced in Scenario #1. You are gaining quality and affording yourself the trial of your product with a better review of content for all responsible parties. That quality and testing will also apply to what gets delivered at the day 30 mark. By allowing the production team to just focus on a few essential elements, you should get better looking, well-tested, and edited content. Then concentrate on updating that content in the first week or two after being live. You'll learn some things to apply to the next round of pages.

Now let's create a more in-depth scenario.

SCENARIO #3
Day 1: Basic three-page site is live—About Org, About Campaign, Sign-Up
Day 30: Donate page live, Blog live, News Releases live
3 Month: Petitions pages live, Events pages live
6 Month: Integration with CRM for volunteer management
12 Month: Basic updates continue

I would recommend looking closely at the goals at each of these time milestones and ask what is flexible. What is essential and what is connected to an external deadline. Every feature you add that involves a database, should be considered very carefully and only chosen according to whether you can do it with one unified database of tools, or if you'll need many.

Real Life Processes: Priorities and Long-Term Solutions

On a major project I am consulting on, we scoped out for an organization that wanted to be doing community organizing. We were able to separate the short-term needs from the long-term needs and create a web development plan from there. The plan looked a little like this:

Day 1: Basic three-page site is live—About Org, About Campaign, Sign-Up
Day 30: Hiring page and other simple info pages up
3 Month: Donate page live, Events pages live, Blog live, News Releases live, Integration with CRM for volunteer management
6 Month: Petitions pages live
12 Month: Build out more in-depth issue pages

In this scenario, the events and data integration were major priorities because the top goals of the organization were to do in-depth community organizing around issues. You might ask, "If those were the top goals, then why didn't it happen in the first 90 days?" It's about being realistic about whether or not something is a real priority. If it needs to work well over time and grow, you should work toward the best long-term solution.

One of the key audiences we needed to build for the first 90 days was comprised of major donors and funders. The initial push for volunteers would happen in three to four months after the first pages needed to be up. In this particular case, we didn't even build the site on the same system, because long term, we would need a well-integrated database that allowed for emailing, volunteer management, voter file data, and petitions.

We decided we would give ourselves the time to set that all up properly. We would start with a light lift, easy out-of-the-box site template, and get basic info out into the world. From there, we would build out the in-depth site we needed later.

This is why knowing the goals for several major milestones is so key. It allows you to avoid rushing work that needs quality time and it ensures you make the right decision on resources both short term and long term.

Website and Web Development: New project

By now, you have some framing on how to think about some key milestones for day one, day 30, three-month, six-month, and 12-month goals. Next, you are going to need to figure out the resources to get there.

The new project. It has you excited because you are kicking off a new campaign! It's going to be the best yet, with bigger goals, a bigger impact and that means you are going to do things like you've never done them before. You are going to build something awesome and new because . . .

Here is your key question: *What is the goal of the web development?*

I've been a part of hundreds of sub-campaign pushes from voter registration drives and email campaigns to corporate targets, photo-petitions, micro-sites for one key message, and launching big campaigns that need a full new site.

In all of these cases, you really need to begin by asking: What is the campaign goal?

From that answer, sub-questions develop:

What do we need to impact to meet that goal?
How have we or others done this before?

Once you answer that, you need to know: For Web Development, our top goal is… and our three sub-goals are [1], [2], [3].

Someone who understands web development should be consulted as early as these campaigns goals are decided. Too many times, I've watched people without web development experience go into planning and get really excited about their ideas. And too many times, I've watched people get wedded to ideas without consultation and (more often than not) the product doesn't meet their goal. The times when web developers have been in the room early on, I've seen it consistently lead to a far better product that meets goals and moves the needle on change.

To make these kinds of decisions, you should be able to make a distinction between the following things:

Website: Any multi-page site on the internet regardless of the functions on the site.

Micro-site: A page with less than five pages, and often as little as one to three pages. And if it has more than three functions, it is probably a small website and not a microsite. If it's hosting images, a donation page, and a sign-up page, that's a website.

Web tool or application: Folks often get confused here and mostly think of phone apps. But this would typically be anything that renders or captures data or allows someone to take an action. Basic web pages typically show static information and images or videos that stay constant unless updated on the backend. If the user can make a selection that renders different data on screen, or submit info that sends to a target, or they have a data-driven profile, web tools or applications are in use. The distinction is they are typically harder to create and manage long-term.

Sub-section of a site: This could have a distinct look and feel compared to the main site. It could even have a different URL that directs you there, but is on the same backend and layout of the site.

These distinctions are critical to proper planning because they clarify the specific resources needed to build and maintain your website.

NEW PROJECT: CAPACITY

It's important to be realistic and carefully consider the tradeoffs. There are always some.

A big question you need to ask: "Is there in-house capacity or do we need to look for outside support?"

If you believe there is in-house capacity, you should know what the trade-offs are. Will it mean holding off on other updates or will basic edits get deprioritized? Make sure everyone is aligned on the tradeoffs.

Here are a few tips:

- Make sure you know how basic troubleshooting is going to happen during the special project phase.
- If you are bringing in outside support limit their point of contact to one or two people. Group calls can be fine but even with just two people you will have some conflicting input.
- An important part of web development timelines is making sure there is time for delays. I've watched many missed deadlines occur because the preliminary deadlines were overly optimistic. Make sure everyone involved has accounted for at least a day of delay at each milestone.

ENGAGE

"You might think that feedback and troubleshooting would all happen during the execute phase, but in reality, many bugs don't appear until projects go live. It's normal. You need a plan to troubleshoot and edit.

BE CLEAR with stakeholders."

Website and Web Development: Rebuilding an Existing Site

Now this is a doozy. I was around for the rebuild of several iterations of BarackObama.com and led RAN.org through two rebuilds in two years. The planning here is very similar to planning for a new organization but with different considerations. A major tip I shared with someone starting a rebuild at another organization: **You need to manage day-to-day operations or manage the website project—don't do both.** Both require a high amount of capacity. Either bring in contract support to keep daily operations going, or bring in contract support to make the site happen. Doing both will most likely mean you won't be able to do either very well.

When rebuilding an existing site, your main question around goals is more nuanced but very similar to what you need on day one.

I've seen minimal iterative design work go well and I've seen it go poorly. When the team relaunched Obama 2012, it was very stripped down and minimal. It did not link to the years of blogs and content the supporters had built up. While that ruffled many feathers, the main goal of giving the campaign a fresh look and feel was achieved by cutting off past content. It gave the press a reason to cover a campaign launch they knew was inevitable because it was a sleek new look and feel for the campaign, and not a sprawling five years of organizing the website.

I recommend having very clear day one, day-30, three-month, six-month, and one-year milestone markers. In a recent relaunch I worked on, we didn't have all of this laid out well, and it meant that the struggle to bring back online organizational resources we needed, became an intra-organizational struggle. Learn from this example and please don't repeat this mistake. Consult with other organizations that have gone through this. Not sharing expectations of when features will return, will create internal turmoil instead of relief of having a modern site. Lay it out on the timeline and take everyone along on the path.

Website and Web Development: Capacity and Planning

We've laid out a few buckets with which to frame the kinds of website development projects you might encounter. However, the only way to make any of them happen is, to be honest, about capacity and planning. Capacity and planning are a bit of a chicken and an egg scenario. They both can dictate what is possible, and one doesn't necessarily come before the other.

Capacity is about internal staff and budget. If these are initial constraints, then start here. If your project is more about scoping, determining budget and answering capacity needed, then start at planning. Here are a few views of realistic capacity as of Fall of 2016:

BUILDING A FULLY FUNCTIONING WEBSITE THAT IS CONTENT RICH.
Working with quality development firms will cost $30,000 and up, and take about three months or more to be done well.

A team of one web developer, designer, content writer, and project manager working full-time on launching a full site might need most of their capacity for three months. That same team with other ongoing projects should have at least six months to work on the project in parallel.

BUILDING A BASIC SITE WITH JUST A FEW PAGES AND FUNCTIONS.
Working with quality development firms will cost around $10,000 and up, and take about a month or more to be done well.

A team of one web developer, designer, content writer, and project manager working full-time on launching a full site might need most of their capacity for a month or two depending on internal review processes. That same team with other ongoing projects should have at least two to three months to work on the project in parallel.

BUILDING AN ACTUAL MICROSITE, OR MAIN-SITE SPECIAL PROJECT, OR VERY BASIC FIRST PAGES OF A WEBSITE.

Working with quality development firms will cost around $3,000—$5,000 depending on visual design and content and will take about a month or more to be done well.

A team of one web developer, designer, content writer, and project manager working full-time on launching a full site might need most of their capacity for two to four weeks depending on internal review processes. That same team with other ongoing projects should have at least three to five months to work on the project in parallel.

Hopefully, the microsite piece helps you understand and plan for concurrent projects if you are at a large or midsize organization running multiple campaigns or projects. Don't plan on more than one special project at a time unless you are bringing in more capacity for development, design and other skill sets, either in-house or via contractors.

Project Planning for Web Development

My recommendation for a process to plan:

Step 1: Know your Goals
Step 2: Scope your project
Step 3: Develop project plan
Step 4: Execute project plan
Step 5: Review goals in relation to the executed project. Learn.

STEP 1: KNOW YOUR GOALS

Make sure you've got the following down:

- You understand your needs and your #1 Goal. You also know the top three subgoals and the long-term goals of the organization.
- You know what needs to happen on the website on day one.
- You know what needs to happen on the website at the 30-day, three-month, six-month and even one year marks.

STEP 2: SCOPE YOUR PROJECT

This is the time to dig into what you really want. It's discussing what is behind the goals of the development and what you want the site to look and feel like. Look and feel aren't some hippy-dippy concepts, they are the cornerstone of User Experience (UX). Take this very seriously—it can make or break a project.

Take time to look at other sites and understand what you like and dislike about their design and function. Make a living document of it. Come together and discuss it.

Then make sure you are working with a qualified web developer and designer who can look at different designs and use that to influence your product. Also, make sure you are all on the same page about intended deliverables.

STEP 3: DEVELOP YOUR PROJECT PLAN

You start with the goals. Then add in the scoping to understand some broad ideas. Scoping should translate into building out a timetable with clear deliverables. I highly recommend having a clear plan that outlines a schedule for mockup review and web development review together in one place.

Make sure you know at each step who is accountable for the deliverables and who needs to review for sign-off. Here are some questions you'll need to answer.

Who is responsible for creating the mockup art for the page?
Who is responsible for choosing or creating imagery for a page?
Who is responsible for the development of the page?
Who must review the content before development?
What is the timeline for that review?
Who is the final decider on a mockup before production?
Who must all review a page after development?
What is the timeline for that review?
Who is the final decider on a mockup before a page goes live?

You should answer those questions in your plan. This should include all of your goals, benchmarks, and milestones. I highly recommend having all of this clearly laid out in your plan. If you are building a large multi-page site these questions will be even more invaluable. Personally, I've watched projects get gridlocked on each of the questions above. If you get gridlocked in a few of those and things become unclear, I promise you a three-month project will become five or six and a scramble to finish. A good plan won't avoid all of that either but will make it much better.

> **TIP:** In planning, you should be sure to include a launch plan. I would make this a separate document from the detailed development plan. But a big mistake I've seen a few times is a lot of thoughtful development work with no launch plan. I'm going to assume if you are reading this, you intend to have an impact no matter what your web development is.

This is the nuanced web that is digital. How do you intend to get people to engage with what you are developing? Is it paid ads, emails updates, earned media, social, media, or a combination? Good analytics can also help you track and plan where you get traffic from.

STEP 4: EXECUTE PROJECT PLAN

Execution is relatively straightforward, but my biggest tip is to be communicative. I highly recommend giving folks a weekly update on progress and where you might be ahead or behind.

> **TIP:** If you are doing a sizeable in-house project that is going to suck up a lot of organizational capacity and don't have a pure project manager on staff, I recommend bringing in one if you can. On redeveloping the site for RAN.org, I often found myself holding some of that role and trading that off with others. That plus other day-to-day functions meant sending the weekly report would slip. It also meant the project pieces would sometimes live in limbo unclear of who had to drive which piece to completion.

You should be tracking your benchmarks and milestones. Update and evaluate as you go. I promise you, being behind rarely changes the deliverable dates in a linear way. That means being two days behind rarely just allows you to shift the deliverable date by two days or add capacity of 16 hours. It most likely means you've learned something about your plan and need to update the overall plan.

STEP 5: REVIEW GOALS IN RELATION TO THE EXECUTED PROJECT. LEARN.

Take time to review your top level goals, benchmarks, and milestones. Are you meeting those goals? Are you getting the change in the world you wanted?

Some questions you should ask yourself for review and reflection:

What did you learn in the day-to-day process? Did you learn anything about what is realistic in development for your organization? Are there elements of communication and approvals that could be improved?

Are the actions happening the way you intended? Are things on the site functioning as you planned? If not, why not? If yes, is there anything you can carry forward into future projects?

Are you getting the world impact you expected? If not, is it a problem of traffic and exposure? Did what you build work for your goals?

An essential part of being able to answer these questions is good analytics on your site. At the most basic level make sure you have google analytics setup so you can at least understand site traffic. I highly recommend setting up the goal function of google analytics to know if the actions you intend are happening where you expect across the site.

Real Life Example: Applying What You Learn

When we re-launched the website for RAN.org, we had planned an everything on the homepage strategy. This design theory had two considerations: First, most websites of action and content-based organizations don't get that much traffic to their homepage; it mostly comes through the action and content pages driven by social and email. Second, eliminating requests from staff and board members who couldn't find a particular thing on the homepage would eliminate repose and conversation time.

To our surprise, after the new site was live and we had a few months of valid data, we realized that 30% or so of our website traffic came through the homepage. This made sense

---

given how much new traffic we were driving via earned media and ads. So we decided to rethink the goals of the homepage and how to be more intentional in delivering focused content that orientated new users to both active campaigns and the organization itself.

Summary

Once you know whether or not to start into a new web development project and if that is the best way to meet the goals, you are off to a well-framed start. It will help you answer which of the following kinds of projects you are digging into:

- For a new organization or campaign
- A new project
- Rebuilding an existing site

With those foundations laid, you can address questions about capacity and resources. With all of that answered, you can start to dig into the structural elements for web development and make sure it all meets your goals.

Stories and Studies

Presented by Jim Pugh and Nick Catalano.

Clear Communication is Key

JIM PUGH // CEO, ShareProgress // www.shareprogress.org

Something that often gets under-prioritized in web development is the importance of good communication. Reaching and maintaining alignment on project vision and scope is critical to web development projects, especially because you often need to bridge a technical and/or non-technical language barrier. I've seen and personally experienced multiple cases where projects that initially seemed like pretty straightforward website builds for a campaign or advocacy effort, ended up turning into very difficult work experiences because there wasn't a solid line of communication between the developers and the person, or people, overseeing the project. If you're involved on either side of a web development project, I would strongly urge you to invest extra effort into communication and ensure you achieve clear alignment on what you're aiming to accomplish.

Five Rules of Tech Security

NICK CATALANO // Progressive Technologist // @NickCatal

Over the past four years, I've been the tech guy behind of some pretty big websites and social media accounts. One of our biggest concerns was someone taking over either one of our social accounts or a staff email inbox, usually via phishing or some other form of online fraud. To prevent that from happening, we followed some straightforward rules—everyone can follow these to keep themselves safe:

Rule #1: Use two-factor authentication whenever it's available. When you use two-factor authentication, you're requiring two sets of credentials to get into each account. The first "factor" is something you know (your password) and the second is something you have (usually your phone, but sometimes a USB or Bluetooth key if you want to be super secure). Using two-factor authentication means that even if you do get phished, an attacker would still need to access your physical device to get into your account, which is way more difficult than just getting your password!

Rule #2: Use a password manager/locker for all passwords, and encourage all staff and volunteers to use it for both work and personal accounts. We chose Last-Pass because it was competitively priced, supported sharing passwords between teams, and has two-factor authentication. Other good options include Dashlane, KeyPass, and 1Password. Make sure to install the web browser extension offered by your password manager. One of the easiest way to spot phishing sites is when your browser extension doesn't offer to auto-fill your username and password like it usually does.

Rule #3: Use strong passwords. Your password manager should have the ability to generate long and complex passwords for you to use on individual sites, but your password manager is only as secure as the password you use for it! I like to follow this XKCD comic (https://xkcd.com/936/) and use random words that are easy for me to remember but are hard for computers to guess. The XKCD tactic is also useful for home wifi passwords, where you regularly need to provide the password to family and friends.

Rule #4: Never use the same password multiple places. If your account is compromised on one website (a common occurrence), attackers can immediately get into all your other accounts that use the same password, and don't have two-factor authentication enabled. Thanks to my password manager, I have hundreds of different passwords, one for each website I have an account on. It's easy and I barely have to remember any passwords!

Rule #5: Only give users who need access to an account access to that account. We've done everything we can to compartmentalize access to passwords to only those who are most likely to need it, and when passwords are no longer needed, we revoke access in LastPass.

Cybersecurity is something everyone should be concerned about, no matter if you run Twitter and Facebook accounts with millions of followers or just talk to your friends over email. And following these simple rules is a great first step towards being more secure online.

 **EMAIL**

E mail is still king. Yes, even with the rise of social media, email is still the leader in engaging, tracking engagement, and empowering engagement.

How to use this chapter

Non-Digital Leadership or Management: It's important to understand good email programs. A strong email list is still one of your strongest assets for engagement and fundraising.

Digital/Tech Staffers: You should know and understand email well. Even if it isn't your core discipline, you should understand how it incorporates web development in landing pages, design for landing pages and in email, copywriting, and data and analytics etc.

New Staff/Activists: You should know this chapter well. If you are building something new email list building can be hard but powerful. Make sure you invest the time.

KEY TAKEAWAYS AND ELEMENTS:
- Identifying goals for email and how to plan for them
- Understanding that email and good content at large is about the "Right Ask, Right Audience, Right Time"
- Determining the value of a subscriber for your organization
- Scenarios and guidance for email testing

- Clear and strategic email structure guidance for different kinds of emails for engagement, fundraising, events, spreading messages, and educating supporters
- A walk through of understanding the importance and structure of data systems, how to use data for more engagement, and expectations from it all

Being such an important part of any program, we are going to use this section to dig deeper into how to think about email planning and theory. We'll go in-depth on structuring the right ask, to the right audience, at the right time. Email testing and structure are key to making the most of your program so we'll make sure you have the knowledge to make good decisions.

The best way to think about digital, is as an ecosystem. To work at scale, a thriving ecosystem means planning for email, social, web development, graphic design, and video working together. Like any ecosystem if the major piece of the ecosystem is off, everything suffers or collapses. Email is often the lifeblood of a good digital ecosystem. If you want to be extremely effective, knowing ads and analytics will take you to that next level.

Email may be the best-documented content stream in the digital space. This section will try to avoid rehashing the best practices you can find in other places and really aim to help you with practical email systems and planning.

One of the best places to get up to date with email best practices is from M+R Benchmarks and their writings throughout the year. The great reporting coming from NTEN.

IDENTIFYING YOUR BEST GOAL FOR EMAIL

You've named your organizational or top project goal. The question should be: *How does email play a part in meeting that goal?*

Whether you are working on a project or a campaign, you need to know the overall goal and the milestone goals for phases. I laid out this theory in an online article by the same name of the theory called the Matrix of Engagement.

The biggest question to solve for in digital engagement is the right ask, to the right audience, at the right time. You have to know both your goals and something about your audience to know you can have a shot at making the right ask, to the right audience, at the right time.

Right Ask, Right Audience, Right Time

Strategic email planning for the Right Ask, is twofold: Does this ask link to the mission and end goal? If people engage in this ask, do they move closer to an end goal or does the organization move closer?

Strategic email planning for the Right Ask, is twofold: First, make sure this ask links to the mission and what you have identified as organizational goals. Secondly, good planning should ensure when people engage in this ask, they either move closer to an end goal or the organization moves closer.

BRAINSTORM AND PLAN

"Right Ask, Right Audience, Right Time (or the three R's) are fundamental to advanced email campaigning.

It's critical to make part of your planning, but takes every step of the engagement cycle to make it possible."

A bad email strategy would look like this:

Email ask >> Engagement >> only completes engagement disconnected from end goal

A good email strategy looks like this:

Email ask >> Engagement >> Action that gets closer to goal

Let's dive deeper. Can you clearly draw a line from the ask in an email to the end goal? If you answer, yes, but… for any one of these reasons:

- *We'll need to deeply explain to people how this ask contributes to our end goal.*
- *We just think this is a good action to keep people engaged, but the direct connection is weak.*
- *Well… it feels like a good action.*
- *Yes we can, but to date it hasn't had the impact we wanted on goals.*

Then, you are closer to a no than a yes.

Good indicators of the right ask also develop over time.

TIP: Build a tagging library. You'll see this again in Data and Analytics. But a tagging library should help you answer: Of the people on our list, who donates and how often? Who engages or has said they like which issues? How often do they engage, and what kinds of actions have they taken to date?

The indicators of the right ask are things like unsubscribe rate, list growth, increased engagement, and making the change you intend to have. Unsubscribes happen for a number of reasons and some have nothing to do with you such as overall email fatigue or change in passion, but most unsubscribes have everything to do with your planning. Unsubscribes can indicate things like whether or not the ask in the email felt disconnected from what they signed up for, that it may have been out of alignment with the values they believed they were aligning with, or they received more email volume than expected.

Real Life Example: Asks and Unsubscribes

Working with a large organization, I believed that launching a monthly newsletter would drive more engagement across campaigns and build more organizational cohesion for supporters. But after a few attempts, the unsubscribes compared to the rate of people sharing it and expanding our list of supporters of one campaign joining another campaign, internally didn't balance out. We were burning off the list trying to get them more engaged. The newsletter was scuttled. It didn't solve for building what we intended and was an indicator we needed a new approach.

List growth from a good ask means you are delivering the kind of engagement people want. Not only are you delivering what people want but they feel compelled enough to engage and share it more widely. When you think of shares of content and actions, it isn't a mere tactical benefit, but an actual validation and benchmark for how much people are willing to endorse your organization.

Increased engagement from people on your email list over time is a prime indicator you are serving up the right kinds of asks. Make sure your email has some ability to look at the health of email open rates over time, actions based on type of action, and actions based on topics of interest.

Email Planning for the Right Audience

The right audience will be tricky and if you are just getting started or simply want to build good data on your email list, then the right audience could be everyone. However, more established organizations and building out good data rarely targets everyone. With good targeting and that specific right audience, you will be able to meet your end goal.

Some of the same indicators to determine the Right Ask, hold true here too such as unsubscribe rate, list growth, increased engagement, etc. You'll want to know what is a good industry or niche average for things like open rates and unsubscribes to gauge if you are connecting to your list. I recommend starting with M+R's benchmarks because they have spent years building datasets from a number of fields on email. Then build data on your own to be able to benchmark how well you are connected to your audience on an email by email basis and over time.

FEEDBACK

"Over time, you can only get the 'Right Audience' if you track your data, compare goals, and use it to start the Planning & Brainstorming phase of the Engagement Cycle again."

The email templates I use in email planning all ask questions of topic, audience, and tactic because those question help think through the right ask, to the right audience, at the right time. To meet short-term and long-term goals, it is important to be thoughtful regarding audience. Here are a few thoughts on how to choose audiences.

First, you need some data. If you don't have any, look at Data Library in the Data and Analytics section of the book and start building data. Every good email program uses data as its backbone.

Second, you'll need to know how large of an audience you need to meet your goal.

One way of determining this is by asking what type of impact you want the audience to drive. Here are a few examples:

HOSTING AN EVENT

I've seen a few examples of organizations want to ask everyone on their list to host an event. While that's not bad once in awhile, data is important because you can hurt overall engagement with a continued ask to the wrong audience. Are there any pieces of data you know about current hosts? Are there any typical actions they take? Are hosts more likely to be people who also attend events? Think about narrowing your audience best on ideas like that. Maybe simple things like first ask your previous hosts and then expanding audiences instead of driving unsubscribes from the bigger list.

Real Life Example: Email Ask to a Specific Audience

Working on a project to eliminate rainforest tree pulp from a major fashion company's supply chain, we wanted to culture jam that corporation's hashtag by taking advantage of it. The plan was to use it to expose the labor issues in their supply chain related to that pulp. We could have asked everyone on our email list to join an action on Twitter, but we knew that Twitter use from the broader U.S. population isn't that high, and we didn't want to bombard a large group with several emails. We suspected based on past data on email unsubscribes, that it may lead to a larger amount of unsubscribes than we were comfortable with. So we changed tactics and analyzed the corporation's hashtag. It looked like they received around 200 to 500 tweets a day on it, so we didn't need 500 to 1,000 tweets like we initially thought. We really just needed to get 100 to 250 tweets to gain the exposure we wanted.

So our main goal was to jam the hashtag. To meet that goal we had a benchmark of tweets we needed to be successful, so the audience we needed were likely people to join this Twitter action. We backed out from the goal of a minimum of 100 unique tweets and we estimated an open rate of 15% and an action rate of 25% so we needed a list of 2,700. We took that 2,700 and asked ourselves: do we think we have some audiences that would be right to ask to join this smaller targeted list? Because we had been building data, we had a list of a few thousand people we thought we could convert a high percentage based on their past engagement with email action related to Twitter. We also then looked at a group of people we had tagged as interested in the issue and were also likely Twitter users. We emailed them to join our culture jam as well. What we ended up with, was the right audience that had opted into getting a series of emails over a few days. They had an average open rate of 30-40% with action rates over 40%. We reduced unsubscribes by targeting our audience according to high open and action rates because we knew these were indicators of the right audience getting the right ask at the right time.

The Value of a Subscriber

Building your audience should be about knowing your goals and what tradeoffs are worth. Let's say a fundraising deadline is looming. Your impulse may be to email everyone multiple times to ask for donations. An important piece of data you need to consider is the value of an email subscriber to your organization. You should use this number to help you answer whether or not expanding your audience is literally worth it in terms of potential unsubscribes.

Two easy questions to help determine the individual subscriber value to your organization include: 1) What is the average email value? 2) If you do paid email list building, how much do you pay per email per year?

If you send test emails (and yes you should always, always test—see section on Email Testing below) then you know the importance of finding the best option for compelling positive action. But you should also think about the cost. To dig into both questions a bit, here are some ways to think about it.

Email value per year is a simple equation of:

$$\text{Total online fundraising in dollars} \div \text{Total number of emails on your list}$$
$$= \text{Average Email Value}$$

In other words, if you raised $200k and had 50k emails on your list, your average value would be $4. So if you were setting an email intended to be a fundraiser, but had 500 people unsubscribe because of bad performance on the email, you lost the opportunity to raise a potential $2,000 from that list of emails that unsubscribed. If your goal was to raise $5,000 from the email send, but you lost $2,000 in potential annual revenue from the unsubscribes, your real net raised would only be $3,000. Now the individual email report wouldn't show that loss because most reporting only shows net raised. Knowing your organizational email value is highly important so you can better assess net cost and real amounts raised.

IMPACT

"Fundraising probably isn't the only goal of your organization. You might want to separate the value of donors, the value of supporters to action, and those that align in the middle."

Paid email cost equation:

$$\text{Total cost of new emails} \div \text{Total number of emails you recruited}$$
$$= \text{Cost per new email}$$

In other words, if you spend $50k in ads to recruit 20k new emails to your list your cost per email is $2.50. If you are sending emails that lead to unsubscribes, is it worth the amount it will cost to get new emails back on the list? Let's say someone in the organization is pressuring you to send an email that performed poorly in tests, and it is likely to lead to 2,000 more unsubscribes. Knowing this value, you could ask them if it is literally worth $5,000 to send the email and, if yes, whose budget would pay to replace that many lost emails.

Email Planning for the Right Time

Right timing is mostly about two things: external factors and internal frequency. External factors include connecting the content to current issue-related calendars or broader external events in the world. Internal timing relates to the number and frequency of emails the organization sends.

ENGAGE

"Multi-year planning and strategy is only possible when you make active choices to engage over time."

Sometimes you have the right audience and right ask, but it comes at the wrong time. Bad timing can cost hours and dollars. Using the list cost above, and factoring staff time coming up short on plans, has real impact. On the fundraising side, I've participated in planning for multiple Earth Day emails that were executed at the right and wrong times. A few years back, there was a last minute rush to get a fundraising email out the door. If you considered yourself an environmentalist and subscribed to several email lists, then you probably received 5-20 fundraising asks that day. The email we sent probably came too late and maybe wasn't our prime day. A year later, we planned to send a fundraiser on a different day. We also decided to ask people to skip the easy donations and take action. It was successful, not just in engagement that day, but in broader engagement because supporters appreciated making the day about action.

Other external factors can be about what is happening broadly related to your issue or the world at large. Holiday weekends tend to be bad days to send emails. Most people are a little checked out from email during major holidays. But being able to sync your email up to breaking moments around your issue, or when your issue has mainstream press, almost always adds positive engagement.

Internal volume can have a big impact on email engagement. Do you consistently send three to four emails a week, or more like one to two every other week? A rapid increase from one a week to four can cause a lot of unsubscribes and might have less to do with the audience and more with the ask. Given the same asks to the same audience at expected time intervals that were more regular between you and your receiver, may have had better engagement and fewer unsubscribes.

Real Life Example: Email and Timing

During my time at Organizing for Action, we had planned a day of action around yet another mass shooting because we wanted to pressure Congress on their continued inaction. Our broad goal was to get Congress to make a vote on some common sense reforms around access to firearms in the U.S. The tactical goal was to get a hashtag trending on Twitter because we wanted to create a national conversation and highlight the congress-people who were still opposing sensible legislation. To do that, we built a number of benchmarks we intended to reach with internal accounts, partners, and supporters. We wanted these conversations to be as noticeable as possible to also attract press to help create a full feedback loop from Twitter to earned media and back to continued social media narrative highlighting representatives blocking legislation.

We emailed a much bigger audience to ask for tweets than I would normally recommend, knowing the overall lower rates of Twitter use compared to Facebook. We believed the theory of the ask and timing might appeal to a larger audience because we knew how passionate supporters were feeling at that time around gun violence reform. It was a success, trending all day, and gaining coverage across most major media outlets. Actually, it was so successful, many people created new Twitter accounts that day just to speak out. One Representative in Texas received so many tweets, he accused us (and namely me) of using digital bots to attack him on Twitter. CNN validated that we just encouraged his constituents to create new accounts to message him. Had we sent such an ask weeks later or prior, I don't believe we would have had that kind of multi-step engagement. It was about making a higher bar ask at the right time.

Email Testing: Always Be Testing

I once interviewed a candidate about how often they think it's necessary to perform subject line tests. They answered when there is time. Wrong answer. Always test subject lines and performance before sending to a broad audience because every percentage point better in open and click rates is a literal shift in engaging thousands of people.

I've been asked a few times how small of a test is worth it. Some might say all sizes, but I do think that 500 is probably the smallest test sample audience you'd want to send to. If you are in a planning phase or only have an email list of 2,000 people, then at the very least you could get a test of two subject lines to two groups of 500 people. Give it at least an hour or two and if the open rates are low, action rates are low, or unsubscribes are high, consider not sending the email.

SOME TESTING SCENARIOS GUIDANCE

Sometimes folks ask what is the minimum number to test and what are some ways to think of list splits for tests. Here are some numbers I've found to be really helpful:

10,000 or fewer people
- Test three subject lines
- Create three groups of 1,000
- Send winning test to remaining 7,000.

100,000 people or more
- You have some space here to be more creative. I would recommend at least
- Test three subject lines
- Create three groups of 3,000
- If one is performing great, send winner to remaining 91,000.
- If not, test two more subject lines each to groups of 3,000

If you are looking at 100,000 people or more I would also recommend some deeper testing like understanding if major cohorts in your emails perform differently. If you have two major tags you wanted to look at specific groups in, I would split this list to also test them.

Test three subject lines
- Create three groups of 3,000 for cohort A
- Create three groups of 3,000 for cohort B
- Send winning test to remaining emails for cohort A
- Send winning test to remaining emails for cohort B

Splitting into further cohorts like that will allow you to learn more about how different groups respond to different kinds of requests and issues. That learning helps you better match the Right Ask, Right Audience, Right Time.

An important thing to remember is you can't test open rate (and sender name) or open rate content at the same time unless you have duplicates. For example, a non-valid test would be sending four different subject lines, but two from one sender and two from another. What would be valid is sending four tests, two subject lines from one sender and the exact same two from another sender. Use the same process if you want to test layout or content. Make sure the layout or content is the same from one sender to the other and they are getting the same subject line.

Always be testing! Testing two items in same test sample = bad test. Focus in on one test at a time.

We've got Right Ask, Right Audience, Right Time. And now you'll always be testing. Let's talk about email structure.

Strategic Email Structure

Every email is unique and the way you plan your email program will change the impact you have. Emails are most powerful when customized to the goal you need that email to achieve. An email can even have multiple goals, but you should avoid more than one ask. A split ask is when you give people two or more options in the email. Here, the paradox of choice kicks in. For every option you add, you decrease the likelihood that action will be taken on any option.

There are occasions where an email could have a split goal for impact. In addition to clear asks and good timing, emails are also about content theory. People start to think of the email audiences as falling into only one bucket like a donor, an in-person activist, or an online activist does. But part of good data is knowing the kinds of actions people will take. The split goal for impact could be both gaining event attendees and letting all subscribers know you are holding live events.

For example, let's say you have an upcoming series of events but the majority of people on your list have never attended an event before. Based on targeting audiences, some might be inclined to withhold a particular audience, such as donors, from the email. However, if hosting in-person events is key to your theory of change and it's important that people know the event is happening, email them all. In this case, the split goal is about both actual event attendance and wanting everyone to know you are fulfilling this part of your mission. You might be okay with a donor or two dropping off because building this narrative for everyone is important.

It's important to know your #1 goal for each email and make that the ask. Are you sending this email to drive online engagement, attend an event, make a donation, spread messaging, update supporters, or educate supporters?

Each of these different goals should actually have a somewhat different format to them. The format should help the reader focus on the intended impact because this is your ultimate goal. The following sections are some in-depth thoughts for specific formatting.

EMAIL FOR ONLINE ENGAGEMENT OR CALLS

I would list in this category things like signing a petition, sending an email to a target, using social media to pressure a target, or make a phone call. These emails should be quick and to the point. You should assume that to some degree, people on your list are connected to your issue or theory of change. Good data can also confirm this to some extent.

IMPACT

"When your actions are online, it can make the Execute>Engage>Impact and Feedback phases faster. Really know your goals and stop email tests that aren't hitting the mark and retest."

Even if it's a new target or topic, but fits your campaign model, get to the action ask quickly and without getting entrenched in the story upfront. When your goal is action, focus on the action and make the execution of it as simple as possible. For example, if you are doing work around gun violence reform and you are driving a petition to a specific governor, then make the ask for a petition signature right up front. Don't spend sentences and paragraphs explaining gun violence or all the technical details of the bill, even if it is a governor you've never mentioned before in a state you haven't previously targeted. People have joined your email list because they trust you to determine if this tactic is the right one for this issue. Just get to the ask of signing and what it is for in the first two or three sentences.

Try to keep these kinds of emails to one to three short paragraphs. The only exception would be if you are making some complicated ask. Most asks like a petition take a minute or less to complete. A longer ask would be something you think requires several minutes of time rather than a minute or less form or quick phone call. Filling out a multistep comment form would be such an example. Tell people how long it will take and why it's important, and you'll see great results.

If you truly believe you need four to five paragraphs explaining an ask, I would question if you have the right audience. For most organizations that have done the work to build an audience and trust two to three paragraphs is all you need for them to complete the ask.

EMAIL FOR FUNDRAISING

One of the most common email types across all organizations is a fundraising ask. Because of this, it is also probably the type of bad email we all see the most. Often, we get a laundry list of asks telling us why to give, or we get an update on everything the organization is doing. Sometimes these laundry lists of emails work and raise some funds, though people who give to these emails are most likely very deeply connected to your organization or issue.

Keep the email about the impact the donor is going to have on the issue. Make it appealing on an individual level. Try to keep it to one topic and, if you can, just one story. For example, one story may look like, lions are killed by poachers every day or so, but Cecil is one lion who stood out because people can personalize with one. Are you working on a water crisis in the U.S. or abroad? Include a fact or two to support your cause but don't give people painful facts to make your case. Give them the human story of one human impacted by the water issue, and let them put themselves in that person's shoes to allow them to be an agent of positive change in the story.

Most humans relate to stories better than numbers, so use facts and statistics sparingly to validate your story. Yes, issue campaigners are often a treasure trove of facts and statistics. Use those in informational documents. Use a good story and one direct ask to fundraise.

EMAIL FOR EVENTS

Keep it about the event, plain and simple. If you need to educate people on the event and issue, you probably have the wrong audience.

Make it timely. For some major events, long-term notice is ok. Otherwise, keep it no more than two weeks out unless it's something people have to book travel for.

Emails like this are typically best formatted as a few sentences about what you are doing. Event details and sign-up are all you need. And if you want, add a paragraph or two of what will happen at the event.

Did I forget important facts and statistics on the issue? No, they don't belong here. I am harping on this because so many organizations litter their content with overkill information that distracts people from taking the goal action.

EMAIL TO SPREAD MESSAGING

This is another simple type of email tactic. Did your organization get awesome press, release a new document in the world, or have a messaging narrative you want to drive via social media? Make it short and summarize why that piece of content is important, not the issue. You should be sending this to people already vested in the organization or issue.

IMPACT

"Sharing messages is an online action. If your email isn't getting shares in testing, STOP sending it. Change something or find another tactic."

Write a sentence or two and share. Maybe a paragraph on why sharing is important to your theory of change and why the reader taking action makes an impact.

That's it.

EMAIL TO UPDATE OR EDUCATE SUPPORTERS

This is your chance to be wonky. Don't confuse this with taking an action or making a donation. If you want to put an ask at the end, that's great, but if the ask at the end is your goal, and you married it under paragraphs of text, you'll probably miss your goal.

These are the kinds of emails where you can break down facts and give some story to statistics. I personally think many people want more of these from organizations separated from other asks. Most people are interested to know more about things they care for. I also believe delivering a few of these over the year can and should have a net positive impact on other actions like petitions, attending events and donating.

Email Planning Guidance

We've covered Right Ask, Right Audience, Right Time. You now know to always be testing. You've got email structure ideas to play with and now, let's plan it all out.

Email planning should be about building a good system in your project or organization to get great content planned, approved, and out to supporters. To make this happen I think it's important to have these items in place: a calendar, layout and approval checks, data and tagging systems, and review and feedback mechanisms.

EMAIL CALENDAR

Keep it simple and make it part of your internal calendaring system. Personally, I love using a google calendar if possible. Create a calendar event for the day it's going out. Include the topic and audience.

In your project space, the minute you have a possible date, add it to your calendar with the intended audience identified. Adding the intended audience always makes it easier to know if an email should be moved a day or not. Were you planning on launching two petitions to an overlapping group? Probably a bad idea because it feels like you are asking a lot in one day. Were you planning on a petition email and an ask to attend a cool local event in one city? It could be okay for someone to get two emails from you the same day if they are added value. If the petition was for an issue someone cared about, followed by an invite to an event hours later, there is likely to be a positive impact to attendance because you'll be fresh in their minds.

Keep what is rapid response rapid, and plan the rest. One of the biggest struggles I've seen in scaling a good email program, is the burden of time when rushed. If a few people need to review an email, give them time to schedule themselves around other work and you'll most likely get a better product than pushing for a last minute review.

EMAIL DRAFTING LAYOUT AND APPROVAL CHECKS

Clearly, the approval checks has a calendar component and it links in well with drafting layout. Make it easy for people to get a good sense of the email content by using a consistent drafting and editing system.

I recommend using a google doc or other shared online document system because they allow for notes and redrafts in the same place. You should include things like audience, email goal, and subject lines all in the drafting document.

Personally. I also like to include landing page text in the same document if there is any reason for a new action or donation page.

When it comes to approvals, I recommend trying to get a system of no more than three or four people that have full sign-off power. Maybe you include someone else for fact-checking, but keep it to who must say yes or no. In my current role as digital director, I don't sign-off on every email. I believe that we hired quality people to create content for the organization so as long as it's been seen by someone with communications and campaign authority on that topic, it's good. I try to review as many as I can, but I work more with my team in looking at trends and performance than grammar editing.

EMAIL DATA AND TAGGING SYSTEMS

I've mentioned much about tagging. I speak from painful experience where I inherited an email program that had three main tags. We had no clue what kinds of actions people were taking or how often. That made it hard to really know who was on the email list and how to get the right asks to people. Most email clients currently have some ability to tag people. I say work with what you have but if you are planning to scale, make sure your system can hold good data over time.

EMAIL REVIEW AND LEARN

Clearly you need data for this. I would encourage you to also make sure you can look at past emails and performance. I would recommend a spreadsheet that has the type of email as well as information about email content performance like open rates, test sizes, unsubscribes, spam rates, and any other metric that helps you learn how to better serve your audience.

I would also encourage you to make it easy to review content. In one role, I had to use NationBuilder, which isn't great for searching for old emails by send. So we forward the winning email plus stats on tests to an emailreport@emailaddress to build an archive with a good date range. It's invaluable to look at real data with real content instead of making guesses about last year.

Use benchmarks for the amount of emails you want to send, and track benchmarks for kinds of emails and outcomes. That kind of knowledge will help you match the Right Ask, to the Right Audience, at the Right Time.

EMAIL EXPECTATIONS

Not knowing the goals the impact for each email will lead to overall less impact.

But less is actually more in regards to stats and facts around issues when the ask is simple. That kind of less will get more impact by not overwhelming the reader.

Email is not a silver bullet to anything. It won't save your messaging problem if you have bad messaging. Or fundraising if you have bad asks. But when you work through good planning around the right ask, to the right audience, at the right time you have the ability to leverage the most effective engagement medium (literally) at your fingertips. That is why email is still king and, done well, it has the ability to change strategic impact across all organizational goals.

Summary

Email strategy starts with making the right ask to the right audience at the right time. Be specific about who your audience is, and know the value of each subscriber using data to determine possible trade-offs. Testing is an easy way to increase open rates and learn more about your audience. Always be testing. The structure of your email will change depending on the purpose of your email, and proper planning will help you gather the data you need to customize your email audiences and improve engagement with your audience.

Stories and Studies

Presented by Amelia Showalter, Jason Rosenbaum and Murshed Jaheed.

The "Ugly" Side of A/B Testing

AMELIA SHOWALTER // Co-Founder and CEO, *Pantheon Analytics* //
@ameliashowalter

One thing A/B testing teaches you is that many of your gut instincts are wrong—but that's okay. Sometimes when you test out a new idea and it fails, you can still learn something valuable. On the 2012 Obama campaign, I had the idea of making our Quick Donate emails look prettier by using nice-looking buttons for the listed donation amounts, instead of the plain text we had been using. But when we tested it, the pretty buttons got us worse results.

So then the question became: should we go the other direction and make things uglier instead of prettier? We decided to run a test where we added ugly yellow highlighting to certain key portions of the text. The result: we got significantly more donations with the ugly yellow highlighting than without. So periodically on the campaign we would add this ugly yellow highlighting to our emails—though, not all the time, since we didn't want to ruin the novelty of it. But it was a good lesson that A/B tests that end in "failure" can actually be inspirations for successful testing in the future.

Unsubscribing Inactive Members to Improve Email Campaign Success

JASON ROSENBAUM // Director of Technology, *Action Network* //
https://actionnetwork.org

Email deliverability is always a mysterious topic. Here at Action Network, I help a lot of progressive organizations, candidates, and others ensure their emails go to their activists' inboxes and not spam boxes, which is crucially important for any digital program. While there are a lot of ins and outs to deliverability and a lot of details you can get yourself lost in, it's actually pretty basic when you cut through the clutter: Only email activists who are likely to engage with your email.

To understand engagement, it helps to put yourself in the shoes of an email provider—Gmail, Yahoo, Hotmail, or whomever. Their job is to make sure no spammy email reaches their customers, while ensuring wanted email makes it through the spam filter. While spam has been around forever, that doesn't mean this is an easy task. Spammers are constantly thinking up new and creative ways to break through spam filters, so it's hard for an email provider to write rules that will effectively do the job. Over the years they have all essentially converged on one solution—email that is "not" spam is email that the recipient interacts with by opening it, clicking it, and the like. And email that "is" spam is email that is deleted or ignored. Email providers use various tools and algorithms to try to predict whether the activist receiving your email is likely to engage with it. If they think the activist will, then it goes in their inbox. If not, to their spam box.

With that in mind, the golden secret to maintaining deliverability is to only email activists on your email list who are likely to engage with the email you're sending them. This can mean only targeting people who've demonstrated through past action that they care about the issue you're emailing about, or only targeting people who live nearby an event you're asking them to RSVP to. But this also means more generally only targeting activists who've engaged with your email recently.

For some email programs I've worked with, this can be as simple as unsubscribing activists who haven't opened or clicked anything in in a period of time, say the last six months. Some tools can do this unsubscribing automatically, or you can do it once a month as a regular manual task. If you have a larger list you can be even more sophisticated by doing something I learned when I was at the PCCC called "testing down the list." For every email that goes out, first test how it will do to a random sample of activists who have engaged with your email recently, as in the last month or so. If the test does well as measured against your historical averages, send it to the rest of the activists who've opened in the last month and then test to those who opened in the last two months. Continue this testing process until you hit the point where activists are no longer responding, then stop.

A lot of the time your email will only end up being sent to your most engaged activists, maybe only the first few tests will come back positive, and you'll end up stopping after that. But every once in awhile, you'll have an amazing email that will make it all the way to the bottom of the list, re-activating thousands of activists with your best material. This method is like a reactivation campaign and an email deliverability technique all in one!

No matter which method you use, the quick and dirty unsubscribing of inactive activists or more work-intensive testing down the list, both will bring results. I've seen numerous programs go from complete blacklisting, with almost 100% of their email landing in the spam box, to back in business using these techniques. They need some time to work—a few months is normal—but if you give them time, you will see results, and going forward, if you keep these techniques going, you should never find yourself having email deliverability problems again.

It's Not an Email List, It's a Community

MURSHED ZAHEED // Former Vice President and Political Director,
CREDO **// http://bit.ly/2pFQbu5**

When Donald Trump was elected, the team at CREDO Action took a moment to breathe, to grieve, and then, we got to work. Within hours, we were already implementing a long-prepared contingency plan to undermine and fight back against Trump's radical right-wing agenda. And by the time he was inaugurated, CREDO's community of activists was energized and ready to fight for progressive ideals.

But it wasn't until the nomination of Betsy DeVos—an anti-gay, anti-trans bigot who had no relevant experience as an educator and did not even attend or send her children to public school—that we learned just how fired-up our members were. In the span of days, our petition to demand that Senate Democrats block and resist the confirmation of DeVos as secretary of education, rocketed over the one million signature mark, all the way to where it landed, at 1,488,560 signers. It was our most popular petition to date, by far.

While there's no doubt that the momentum of the moment played a huge part in the incredible success of this petition, it's impossible to overstate the importance of treating the people who receive your emails as members of a community—and not just as numbers on an email list—to create engaging activism. When the world is burning down around you, it's easy to fall into the trap of taking your community for granted by focusing on numbers over engagement. But organizations such as CREDO, take the challenge of informing, mobilizing and organizing its members, very seriously.

That means that everything is a strategic and well-oiled digitally savvy organization, publishing with a purpose. Every email, every Facebook post, every tweet, every text message serves strategic objectives and carries a strong theory of change. The idea is that engaging with this content—be it a petition, call request, event invite or even something on social media—can actually accomplish what it says, and is not just shouting into the abyss.

Each campaign CREDO launches, is carefully considered, deeply researched, and often reviewed by its grassroots activists working on the ground on the issues its community is talking about. CREDO's allies across the progressive movement, who are often also CREDO grantees, help the team understand the nuances of what's happening, why it's happening, and how a community of over five million people, can bring their power to bear in the most productive way possible. You can see this careful attention to detail on every email CREDO sends out, which is heavily footnoted with a list of references from reliable sources that range from progressive media to members of Congress.

And before CREDO delivers its content, it takes great care to polish outgoing work—this means each piece of content goes through multiple levels of approval, is proofread, and tested repeatedly to ensure it works.

Don't forget what comes next: CREDO's team members read every email its members send back, and consider how their feedback can inform further activism on each campaign, or future campaigns. It takes a tremendous amount of time and team resources, but if we expect members of an email community to read and act on the emails we send them, they deserve the same respect.

Ultimately, Betsy DeVos was confirmed as secretary of education, but after delivering CREDO's petition signatures—and over 105,000 phone calls—to Congress, we came within just one vote of stopping her confirmation. And since then, the more than one million people who joined CREDO's community, have helped bring their fierce advocacy to other campaigns, like forcing racist white nationalist Steve Bannon off the National Security Council and out of the White House, ending the confirmation process of an anti-LGBTQ bigot for Army Secretary, stopping Trumpcare, and more.

At the end of the day, we should always keep top-of-mind the fact that the emails we send each day are going to millions of real people. It is these people and the vibrant, diverse community they make up, that make our work for progressive change possible.

 # DESIGN

Strategic design is fundamental to communication and engagement. Yet, again and again, I see design being the underfunded and unplanned part of projects, organizations, and campaigns. We are going to dig into why you need to be strategic with planning and funding good design, and then how to plan for it.

How to use this chapter

Non-Digital Leadership or Management: If you haven't invested in design, read this chapter to understand why you should.

Digital/Tech Staffers: Practical knowledge for you to better understand design and how to work with good design and designers.

New Staff/Activists: It's helpful to understand that good design is hard and can be costly, but you can understand it and look for support.

KEY TAKEAWAYS AND ELEMENTS:
- A clear case for why an investment in design is an investment in engagement
- Practical advice on how to plan design
- A breakdown of how to design for logos and branding
- How to design for website planning tips
- How to design for social media planning tips
- Design for print planning tips

Good design crosses all platforms and mediums. It gives an emotional element to your work that shifts your appeal from just an issue or a person to a feeling. Humans are more powerfully moved by feelings than facts. If you can combine compelling facts and reason with design that is appealing, you'll have more compelling content with a level of engagement that can help lead to major wins.

Story: Great Design Works

When I accepted the role at RAN (Rainforest Action Network) one of my biggest concerns was design capacity and making the budget case for a talented graphic designer. I've seen a number of organizations think of design as a nice thing to have, instead of a must-have when it comes to capacity and budget. I believe it comes from a misunderstanding about what moves people and the true impact of design in connecting with people by inciting emotions and feelings.

I had the pleasure of working with very talented designers and design teams at all of the Obama organizations I worked with. Working with talented designers, it was powerful to see the impact of proper design to make content engaging, and often more clear, either in simplicity or legibility. Those designers would take rough mockup ideas campaigners presented them with, and they engaged in the art side of digital for impact. On the flip side, I've seen a number of campaigns and NGOs expect design to be voluntary or just a thing someone with Photoshop can do. There are a lot of skillful self-taught designers out there, but just having a design tool doesn't make someone a designer any more than buying a stethoscope makes me a Doctor.

I was delighted when I found out we not only had a Senior Art Director who focused mostly on print, special event design, and overall brand design management, but we also had an in-house designer, Jake Conroy, focused on website and social media design. But because of some unclear planning, his designs weren't being consistently used on social media. The Facebook page was in moderate shape with 80k likes. By employing consistent content design that allowed a very talented designer to do what he does best, the page started on a trajectory of sharp growth in likes and engagement. We mixed his good design with consistency in frequency, timing, and quality of content. Within a few months, we rushed passed 100k likes—a growth rate of 25%. Empowering the designer to drive smart and engaging design, we saw a number of posts getting hundreds of thousands of impressions converting into new fans which meant more people signing petitions, taking actions, and connecting with the organization. Over the following year, the page tripled in size, much of that growth directly attributable to good and consistent design.

A Case for Design Investment

Good design is essential to good campaigning. As noted above, design empowers communication and engagement, two of the most fundamental building blocks of digital strategy. But in a world with tight resources, it is understandable you might find yourself needing to make the case for investing in design. I know I have, so let's walk through some tangible value to design.

Here are a few of the direct values of good design:

Consistent design reinforces your brand and builds the connection to your organization, campaign, or cause. Think about the Obama O, the Hillary H, World Wildlife Fund's panda, or the Twitter bird. Their consistent design from branding to content builds relationships with their audiences.

Good design makes your content engaging. If you intended to engage people in your cause or campaign, this investment will go a long way. This is exactly why major companies will spend millions of dollars on a single design campaign.

Good design creates value you can get a return on. There is multistep and direct return.

Multistep return would be when good design increases Facebook engagement. Increased Facebook engagement leads to more signatures on a petition. You then receive a direct organizational value when those emails later convert to donors.

Direct return comes when you invest in good design for images placed in emails. I've seen well-designed images in fundraising emails perform between 10-30% better than emails without well-designed images.

How to Plan Design

Planning good design gets back to knowing your goals. What exactly is your goal and intended impact?

The best design comes with parameters. Not all design needs to be out-of-the-box. The best brainstorms and creations happen with clear guidelines. Designing for effective campaigning is all about achieving goals.

The best parameters also define scope, which is a way of asking—what exactly do you need?

You should be able to identify the medium, volume, audience, and ultimately the impact you need from a piece of design.

Medium: Here we are defining medium as a channel of communication. This could be a really wide range of things like print for a billboard, tri-fold handout, or black and white flyer. Design for a social media platform has specific sizing parameters. Website design could include an image for a feature area, image in a blog or email, or even a full page. Medium is important because it creates a good initial guide for choosing size, space, color, the complexity of the graphic, and the written content.

BRAINSTORM AND PLAN

"All content has a target audience. Too many organizations say, 'our supporters' without being clear what that means. Get as clear on your design audiences as you would for email or video."

Volume: This is the variance in design production you need. If you need a design to appear on just a flyer, that is a very different project than if you want a similar feel on a piece of content that appears on a billboard, video, blog, and flyers. It could also be volume of related pieces like having 10 social media images for a new campaign. Volume changes planning and capacity a lot. You should make sure the volume matches the goals of the campaign.

Audience: This is who you intend to engage. Different groups of people respond to design in different ways because of personal and cultural taste preferences. There really isn't 'good' universal design because it is inherently subjective. What can feel old and stale to one group could feel comfortable and assuring to another. There are a few ways to approach designing for communities. Approach one, is working with a designer that is from the community you intend to reach. The other is research and understanding what contemporary design looks like on online channels and other mediums that resonate with your audience.

On a deeper design level, if you want to be powerfully engaging, you should be able to talk about the feeling and characteristics of the design. The feelings and characteristics you want the design to have should directly portray the feelings you want it to evoke. For example, if you want your message to be strong you may consider using hard angles as opposed to more curved edges that often get portrayed as soft. Being able to portray feelings that clearly represent your message is a great way to efficiently expedite good design.

Feelings of Design

Working on the National Day of Service—a combined event as part of the Obama Presidential Inauguration and service in honor of Dr. Martin Luther King—I had the honor of working to facilitate the brand design. I worked with the team planning the overall events along with the in-house designer. We went through several rounds of iterative design because of mixed ideas about the feeling of what we needed.

Our first draft felt rustic and classic. The designer and I kicked around some ideas and she designed fantastic mockups, pulling from vintage gasoline company sign designs. These were designs people knew and had seen portrayed in classic events. She added in some texture to make it look weathered and classic.

In review, folks "liked" the designs but it wasn't quite what they asked for. The reality is they hadn't really dug into what they were actually asking for and were describing surface feelings without any depth. They had imagined some of the depth already but didn't express it. We were able to then get deeper descriptions of more institutional classic feelings like something that might fit within the categories of retro pentagon, boy and girl scout merit badges or National Park feelings.

Now we were cooking. The designer and I kicked around a few ideas to see if we were distilling the same ideas from what we were hearing. The luxury of a good designer is someone who can listen and turn what is heard into feelings evolved by their design. What we came back with was a few options that were, in reality, easy to sort through. Combining some final elements, we were able to move forward with the brand and subsequent materials.

With a broader overview and some of the right questions to ask on design, let's dig in on a few tips for specific kinds of projects. One overarching tip to keep in mind is that design is subjective. Being clear about parameters and expected outcomes will get you to an ideal outcome faster.

Design for Logos and Brand Planning Tips

Logo and brand identity are key to overall organizational communication. They should (over time) reinforce who you are, what you do, and in themselves tell a micro story. Logos and design tell this micro story by drawing on feelings and identities to related organizations or projects and the connection people have to your work. This micro story is a segue and an element of the start of all communication from your brand. Here are a few ways to think about brand identity to make sure your design meets your goals.

Designing for logos and branding can be crucial to the life of a project, organization, or campaign. One important thing to remember is designs can evolve. While I wouldn't recommend constantly going through major overhauls, if you are just getting started, don't feel like what you start with is the final iteration. Establish a design that conveys what you want and let it evolve as people interact with you.

Be clear on your scope and the outcome of what you need and can afford. Working with clients and designers, I am always careful to be real about the amount of revisions expected and the complexity for which we have time or budget. Each revision is costing you direct funds paid to design teams as well as organizational time, taking away from work on other projects. I've worked on projects where we were clear that with a particular deadline and budget, we could do stylized font plus a predetermined shape. It is all about matching up the resources available to the goals.

Be clear on how you want your project portrayed. Establish how you want to be viewed by people who will be supporters and those you wish to influence. Are you a young upstart or are you a modern and strong institution? At the end of the day if you don't define it, someone else will. A style guide is a simple document that helps make sure everyone involved is part of building brand consistency.

IMPACT

"Logos have an impact. And it's OK to change yours. It can even be helpful if your core mission or audience are shifting. If you aren't getting the intended impact from your organization's design, use that feedback and plan again."

A complete style guide should have the following:

- Guidance on how to use and place the logo.
- Organizational fonts for logo, organizational name, print and online text.
- Organizational color palette.
- Alternate use colors for logo if needed for black and white and simplified use for stencils

Take time to establish the right feelings and make sure your brand resonates with people the way you intended it to. Then make sure you build out a style guide for brand consistency.

Design for Website Planning Tips

Website design is a robust and often complicated process. Websites for campaigns, non-profits, and activism projects are often part storytelling, part action, part resource center, and part information for various audiences. The sheer scale of complication of all those pieces means you should treat your design process with the diligence it needs to meet your goals. Here are a few more tips for success.

Know what you are trying to design. Is it a full website or a page or feature? Be sure to select a designer that has worked with a project of the scope you need. The exception would be if you are willing to go through the time and process for someone to learn during the build.

Make sure you have designs that work for desktop, mobile, and tablets.

Make sure the designs work in a functional way.

Look at other websites you admire and, in the design process, ask a developer how complicated and expensive features you like are. It's kind of like pointing at a Tesla and saying you want that when you have the budget for an electric scooter. Good planning makes sure you align realistic outcomes with your budget.

BRAINSTORM AND PLAN

"Look at sites you like and admire and try to distill what it is that works. Saying the whole thing is rarely helpful to working it into your design."

Design for Social Media Planning Tips

Great social media often includes great design. There are certainly outliers of accounts that get by with minimal design, but those are the exception. Most engaging accounts take the visual medium seriously and so should you. Make sure you are planning out social media in a way that meets organizational goals but doesn't sacrifice one-time aks for long-term engagement. Here are tips for the planning process.

Make sure you know the platform and where it is going. A Facebook event image is different than an image you want to autoload for a blog and it is also different from a share graphic.

BRAINSTORM AND PLAN

"Design for the platform. Create the right size for Facebook, Instagram, Twitter, etc.

It's even OK if different channels have slightly different styles and feelings. They often reach slightly different audiences."

Test. Social is a great place to test what resonates. Track your social content over time and use that to influence your design.

Let images be images. I mean, don't try to cram every word onto an image. Yes, sometimes you see an "image" that is just text. Rarely do those outperform simple text and compelling images.

Use images to lead and be honest about what comes next. People don't like clickbait. Let an image be real about what they will find from your report, action, or article.

Reuse. Yes, people will likely engage again with your content even if they've seen it before. Repetitive branding is even good.

Keep your social media design authentic to your overall brand and messaging.

Design for Print Planning Tips

My experience over the years is that print designing, while it used to be the staple, is less common for most of us in the campaigns and nonprofit space because of the rise of digital. I'm including it here because it comes up as an ask for most graphic designers. The reality is, most designs that work great for the internet don't translate perfectly to print items like T-Shirts, flyers, and posters. So make sure you plan well for these separately if they are part of your goals.

Really, really know your specifications here. I've watched a number of folks feel good about design and have it look and read horrible once printed.

If this is a new space for you or the designer you are working with, lean on templates. Getting the print margins or look of a large sign correct is rarely easy.

If you are working with a print shop, ask them upfront for all the print specifications.

BRAINSTORM AND PLAN

"Follow print specs very specifically. What looks sleek online can be a mess when you try to just 'use' it on a billboard or t-shirt.

When in doubt, hire out."

Summary

Strategic design is essential for communication and engagement. Knowing the parameters medium, volume, and audience you need to design for will help make sure you meet your goals. Using those parameters as guidelines you can make be certain to use resources well and make an impact in the world.

Stories and Studies

Presented by Jake Conroy, Dan Carson and Jillian Maryonovich.

Using Design to Push for the Weird

JAKE CONROY // Activist, Designer, and Writer // @_jakeconroy

As a designer, I never thought my struggle with staying creative would be with someone besides myself. However, working with nonprofits has been one of the biggest stumbling blocks in keeping my design interesting. The desire to change the world is an important and potent one, and often campaigners approach that from the left side of the brain only. Mixing creativity with messaging comes off as a risk not worth taking. As a designer, it's often an uphill battle to get permission to make something look good; to convince campaigners that looking good actually is effective activism.

Such Sisyphean tasks are often relieved by falling into safe design practices and repetitive elements we know are going to make campaigners happy. So when it was time to boost our social media presence by hundreds of thousands of people instead of tens of thousands, I relied on my supervisor's support to go to bat for me. We tried new things, created interesting content; we didn't stick to the straight and narrow, the tried and true. We stumbled, and failed at times. But the graphics and videos that knocked it out of the park, the ones we still reuse years later to similar success, were those that were most out of left field. The pieces that didn't quite fit the mold of the organization, the ones that celebrated the unique, the ones that received over one million views and took our following into triple figures.

Those successes are the ones that continue to remind me to be the odd one, to invest the time into making the elements and flair that most people will probably overlook, and to always push for the weird, the unusual and the artistic over the left side of the brain that pesters you to stay on the monotonous target.

Busting Design Myths

DAN CARSON // Head of Design and UX, *Crowdpac* // @okdan

Designers have a tendency to hold fast to myths, which can be detrimental when operating in a results-oriented industry like politics. I'd like to bust a few of them in the hope that design can be seen as a skill set distributed across an organization or campaign, rather than as a service deployed selectively by experts.

Myth 1: Designers are the most creative people in the room. In my 14 year career, often times the best idea came from someone other than a designer on the team. When we were designing the volunteer engagement platform on the 2012 Obama campaign, we were focused on utility and the complex tools required to keep our campaign running. But along the way a volunteer noted that we were losing a sense of joy among the volunteers who were actually using the platform. Afterall, their energy was the only reason we'd be able to succeed. So we added a page where you could view a randomly-selected inspirational video of President Obama from the campaign trail. That's it. No likes, analytics, machine learning, or anything else. Just a button to deliver you a moment happiness. And no designer came up with it.

Myth 2: Designers' gut instincts know what will perform best. There are simply too many examples to list here, but I've seen dozens of A/B tests humble me into knowing that my instincts aren't always right. Whether it's colors, copy, or button placement, you have to be willing to be wrong and not take it personally.

Myth 3: Simple is always better. Designers often want to simplify things as much as possible. Cleaner, more whitespace, less friction, fewer steps, etc. But what looks simpler on the surface can do a worse job at helping your supporters achieve their goals. More steps in a donation flow often performs better because each step has the space to contextualize and increase focus. More words explaining what comes next is always better than a clever (but vague) icon. So while the principles of good visual design shouldn't waver, how those principles are applied to a user's journey through your website should allow for what seems like complexity, but is in fact clarity. I'm reminded of the world-class design firm IDEO where I first heard this guiding principle on creativity and design: "Strong opinions, weakly held." It hasn't served me wrong yet.

Designing for the President

JILLIAN MARYONOVICH // Founder and Creative Director, *Sweet Spot Strategies* // @jackrelax

Creating successful, eye-catching, meaningful work is hard. When your boss is Barack Obama, and your client is the United States, it's even harder.

Barack Obama was the first president to really embrace social media and the first to have an Office of Digital Strategy outside of the communications and traditional press offices. Being the Obama White House Creative Director was the most challenging and rewarding job in my life. When I first got hired to work for the Obama Administration, I imagined a rigid, strict and quiet environment. I couldn't have been more wrong. Our team of 20 people who ran Digital Strategy were some of the brightest, hardworking, hilarious, and creative people on the planet. We were all so unified having one objective in our work: Sharing the message of Barack Obama and The White House to the world. (No big deal.)

Balancing best practices for social media while visually displaying the spirit of the message and remaining authentic was a daily, if not an hourly challenge for me. Our main goal was to communicate complex policy topics to the nation and keep our messaging relatable for real people. Our real gut check was "are we delivering a message in a way that would make sense to our parents back home?" If not, we had to rework it. I had to constantly switch gears from displaying data, or explaining the highlights of a new bill, to needing to be agile and respond to a national tragedy like a terrorist attack. I also did a lot of branding, motion graphics and event design for the myriad of White House events and summits that happened daily.

There was such a legacy of historical assets and design that I had to respect but also blend in the upbeat, modern and positive Obama tone. Luckily they (who's they I guess?) trusted me a lot to push the boundaries and craft my own visual take on one of the most known brands in the world.

Our team all definitely hit our limits and spent some nights crying in a basement bathroom (or maybe that was just me.) The stakes couldn't have been higher. If we screwed up, it would be on the chyron of CNN within the hour. If we missed a beat, it could become a national scandal. But we thrived on the pressure. We roller skated in the hallways, we had life-size mannequins of Abraham Lincoln in our office for Halloween, and we all had about six pairs of "fancy shoes" under our desks at all times. We mostly all laughed, sweat, and worked our hardest for this President, this job, and this team, every day. And I would do it all again in a heartbeat.

My main takeaways from this experience:

- Care about your work. Having a rewarding job with a clear mission makes all the hours worth it. If you don't believe in what you are doing, you are doing the wrong thing.
- Have a team you can trust, and then trust them back. Micromanaging is never the answer.
- There will always be people a billion times smarter than you. But you are there for a reason. Recognize your skill set because it is a necessity to keep the machine running.

- No one has their shit together. The person who shows up with a plan will be the one who is heard. Leadership requires risks.
- NEVER READ THE COMMENTS.

 **VIDEO**

Video, possibly more than any other medium, is consistently confused for the goal when it is more accurately a tactic and a medium. For Example, "make a viral video" is not a goal.

Whew… got that out of the way.

What is the goal of the video you intend to make? In this section, I will break down some of the questions around goals because increasingly, videos are accessible and made by lots of people. That doesn't mean they should be made by just anyone with your logo on it. This chapter will outline the elements that help you to resourcefully produce a high-quality video.

How to use this chapter

Non-Digital Leadership or Management: This chapter will help you understand the importance of video, and that good video is as complicated (and can be as costly) as web development projects.

Digital/Tech Staffers: Practical knowledge for you to better understand and leverage video in strategy. Clear process and tips to create great video that drives engagement.

New Staff/Activists: Practical tips you can leverage. While professional video can be expensive, you can still create compelling video with smartphones and basic video tools.

KEY TAKEAWAYS AND ELEMENTS:
- Strategic video with planning for view-based goals and video as a means to impact other goals
- Video Launch Plan that includes goals and tips
- Methods for generating views and thinking for social media, email, website and online ads
- Tips on how to work with partners and celebrities
- How video strategy should go with earned media
- Production Tips to help you plan and create better video

If your goal is to educate, raise awareness, inspire, raise engagement, or build brand identity, these could be good goals for a video. More than other very intensive digital tactics, video can be hard to measure for concrete goals other than views. Yes, you can measure post view impacts, but getting views first takes strategy. Even having one of the goals above doesn't always mean the investment in video is a good idea. Video is a great investment when you've made a decision on the tradeoffs between making a great video and other forms of content. Making sure video is a conscious and well thought out decision is the best way to meet any goal.

Where I would highly caution against video is when you want it as a means to quickly reach another goal directly. For example, if you want video to increase signups for one activity, donate right now, take an action right now, then it probably isn't the best tactic. There is overwhelming science behind low rates of watching a video to its end, and even lower post-viewing action rates. But if you see video as a step of engagement to impact goals, that is a viable strategy. Video is about storytelling and persuasion, and if your goal is to connect deeply with your audience, then it is a tactic worth investing in. I'll expand more on this below.

This chapter is broken down into a few sections:
- Video with View-Based Goals
- Tips on Making Video Work
- Video to Impact Other Goals
- Video Launch Plan: Goals and Tips
- Video Planning: Production Tips

Video with View-Based Goals

You have a goal and it is to educate, raise awareness, inspire, raise engagement, or build brand identity. The first two questions should always be: Is video the right medium? And, do we believe we are equipped to achieve the reach we want?

Is video the right medium for achieving your goal? If you are trying to raise awareness or education on a topic, could this be better achieved through a series of blog posts? Could it be achieved through a series of social media share graphics instead of one longer video? Could it be achieved with a content-rich special page or website? Quite often people want to leap to video because it is a familiar medium most of us grew up with and are immersed in daily. But the ubiquitous nature of video doesn't mean it is always the best way to educate when you consider the many aspects of video. For example, if audio is important to the video working, you are really limiting the audience to when they have the freedom to listen to the video.

Don't rush to reject other content mediums because you want a video. Video requires a large investment of resources so you want to make sure you're intentional with your goal for using video as a tactic. Look at your video view rates vs. overall content consumption rates. Which is more likely to move the needle for you to help you reach your end goal?

Another aspect to consider is whether or not you are equipped to get the reach you want. I'll expand more below in launch plans, but essentially you want to ask: do you have an audience now or do you need to build one to get the views you need? Think about your email and social media reach, and average engagement. If email and social media are the video distribution avenues that you are working with, then consider that many videos only achieve 30 seconds of views via social media. Do you have the infrastructure of reach already in place to have the impact you hoped for? There is a major difference in hoping and

EXECUTE

"Great video execution is hard. Even with increased technology.

Make sure you have the capacity to actually execute your vision."

planning for success. Knowing the target you need to hit and figuring out how to hit it, is what a plan with good strategy should do.

If it isn't social media and email alone, you should think about the budget needed to get views via online ads. Other strategies could and should include using allies and people connected to your organization with their own social media and email reach that would also drive the video. Don't let your email list size and social media reach be the block if you have good content that drives important goals. You should leverage all of your reach to get it out there.

If you don't currently have the audience to drive the views, but you want to create a video that will serve as background content on an issue for the next twelve months, that is a good use of video. You have a clear intention for the video and feel good about the long-term investment that it doesn't matter you aren't going to get the views you need now. An informational video is a great way to give your content a longer life-span.

I love video and think most organizations can invest in it differently. Using video as a piece of well-planned messaging in an Ecosystem of Content, you'll find there are many, many good uses for video. Good video engages in storytelling, it follows formats and formulas, and it is clear about message of both story and action.

Tips on Making Video Work

Outlined below are video planning tips for using video to educate, raise awareness, inspire, raise engagement, or build brand identity. If you are intending to shift behavior, you should either be following a storyline arc or a clear explanation arc. There are volumes and volumes of work on creating good storytelling videos. Here are some of my favorite elements to consider:

- Agreement
- Context—Problem/pain and vision of solution
- Story
- Connection
- Description
- Realization of solution—how
- Call to action

If you need to create explanation videos, I highly recommend picking up the book, The Art of Explanation. It is made by the creators of Common Craft videos. If you are new to video, don't just say "Ah! I get it." Just pick up a copy of their book and I promise every video and piece of content you make thereafter will be better.

Good videos can orientate a person to an issue and give them a connection to either the problem or the solution makers. It's not easy to track if an action successfully follows a video view since there are usually multiple paths that lead to an end goal. For this reason, you can either think about video as valuable for brand building and identity connection, or you can carefully time the release of the video to see if it creates a surge in actions toward an end goal.

If you have the capacity to invest in video, think of it beyond an immediate return. When a video consistently appears, even for a few seconds in your followers' Facebook and Twitter timelines, then you are building a narrative. That narrative should be around the work you engage in. Even if someone isn't watching to completion, it might be enough to continue to keep your organization front of mind for people.

And now for your video tips!

TIP 1: Know your goal and target audience. Goal should be simple like we need to share the story of x community or we want supporters to get a consistent update from our Executive Director.

Audience: It's best to pick just one. When you try to appeal to too many audiences, your message gets lost. You should be able to say we are appealing to current supporters, potential new supporters, a particular target group, or an entirely new audience. It's best to be specific.

TIP 2: Be real about your intended impact of each video. Don't imagine this is going to be "viral," because that would mean your video is being shared to new audiences that you don't normally interact with. Those are audiences you probably aren't the most informed on, making it hard to predict success.

TIP 3: Pay the proper cost. Quality video can be expensive. A short two minute to five-minute piece done by a professional firm can cost $5,000 for some basic work. It's likely to cost north of $20,000 if it involves animation, a lot of interviews, or filming on different locations. Those are fair rates for talented professionals. You can find cheaper and you should make sure what you see in a contractor's reel is what you want.

TIP 4: Stop over-analyzing the transition or exact sound at a certain moment. If you aren't a videographer then trust them. The biggest impact you can make depends on big-picture message and feel. If you are obsessing over little things, you are probably off track.

TIP 5: Audio, audio, audio. If you are trying to do in-house video, invest in audio gear. If you have good audio, you can always add static images or graphics behind it. There's very little that a video editor can do for bad audio. High-quality voice overs can go a long way.

TIP 6: Think about the cuts. If you are investing in one larger video, can you also make shorter cuts to add quality volume to social media? The answer is usually, yes.

TIP 7: Lighting. You don't need an expensive kit but just knowing the basics of good lighting will take a modest video to a more professional level.

Video as a Means to Impact Other Goals

Imagine your goal is to get immediate sign-ups for an event. You or someone in your organization deeply believes that a video is what will do the trick. I've been down this road several times in the multiple Obama related organizations, and at RAN. To date, the data has always pointed to the video decreasing net sign-ups. The reason is similar to the paradox of choice: having to make a decision on either thing also makes you more likely to do neither thing.

Think about it this way—you want to get someone to a piece of content so they can watch all of that content. Then you want them to take a direct action like donate, sign up for an event, or maybe commit to a longer form of volunteering. Your intuition tells you that more information is more likely to get them to sign-up. I get it—on an intuitive level it makes sense, but to date I have yet to see it bear that kind of fruit.

In several cases, it does make strategic sense to pursue video to impact other engagement goals. These instances would be when it isn't the primary or only way to meet the goal but you are using video as a piece (or pieces) of content in a broader Ecosystem of Content. Times when this make sense are:

- You have an abundance of capital for the project and you can layer in video.
- You have an abundance of video production capacity.
- The goal is not possible to meet with email and direct social media asks alone, so you layer in video as supplemental content.

> **ENGAGE**
>
> "Video has the power to drive deeper long-term engagement and even stir people to action.
>
> But when you have a direct ask, try other tactics before you plan videos as your main way to engage."

Let's dig into the latter, layering in video as supplemental content. Whatever the main ask is that you need to convert on, make sure you have built simple pages that make it easy to convert to that ask from email and social. If you know preemptively that you'll never get the conversions you need, then you should be thinking about how to engage people more broadly and this is where video fits in.

Here is where it would make sense to develop engaging video content as a supplemental ask. Very specifically, you would use the video as an engagement hook and link to that action you need conversions on. You could even build out a secondary action page that includes video and an action. Don't make that combined action and video page your main push because, as described above, the paradox of choice will almost always suppress both. Make it a piece of a broader push to build out a full Ecosystem of Content around the action, and one of many ways people can connect to the action. Using video to impact another goal in that way is strategic and will help get you the conversions you are looking for.

Real Life Example: Videos Register Voters

One project I worked on where video made sense to drive a specific goal was for voter registration in Nevada during the Obama 2012 campaign. We had a staggeringly large voter registration goal and we had the amazing luxury of online voter registration. A place where tweets and video links to registration make a very real difference.

We had in-house video capacity because we were lucky to have recruited Tiffani Davis to come out and join us and we had strong statistics on how many voters per hour someone registered. Based on past experience, we estimated three in-person registrations an hour. It's hard to do voter registration for more than a few hours, so a single person might be able to get 10 to 12 registrations before tiring. So we broke down the numbers and realized if we got 3,000 or more views on a video, we felt confident it may translate to 30 registrations (at an estimated rate of 1% conversion to registration). We had the social media means and some noteworthy spokespeople in the state available to us, and we knew if we could turnaround two videos a week with that as the baseline goal, then we could reach people in a way we wouldn't otherwise. Video as a tactic made sense, because it was a piece of content in a broad ecosystem. There would be a volley of tweets, blogs, Facebook, posts, and apps driving registration.

Given the power of shifting the electorate and knowing that we were peaking on the number of people we could register in-person with our resources, video made sense. We were able to identify our goal, audience, and intended outcome, and the clarity of all drove our success.

Video Launch Plan: Goals and Tips

Now that you have some tips on video production for advocacy at large, let's talk about a launch plan. I've actually been part of a few projects where a video that was reasonably expensive got greenlit in one department without figuring out a launch plan.

A launch plan is about how you are going to get views on the video, and it needs to start with the goal of the video.

Know your intended audience because the video should be all about you reaching them. If the rest of the plan doesn't add up to you reaching that audience, you don't have a strategic plan, plain and simple.

So you know your goal and your intended audience. Now you should know how many people you intend to impact with the video. If you can't answer with a target impact, you probably shouldn't be making the video or pushing for it until you can. Know the impact you want to make and you are on the right track to creating and launching a successful video.

Real Life Example: Video Audience

At Rainforest Action Network, an idea came up to develop a video that was orientated around a few major donors of the Executive Director giving an update. The idea was pitched to me with hesitancy. Most of the hesitation was coming from the idea it may be an overuse of resources for a small target.

I suggested we create a plan for a video that focused on two overlapping audiences with the major donors as a subset of general supporters. I don't think this video will get a massive amount of views but we were at a point where developing more organization-wide narrative beyond just the campaigns, was a priority. We believed engaging more people as supporters, of not just individual campaigns, but supporters of the organization, would make it easier to transition more people to new campaigns and give us increased capacity over time. But if this video were part of an ongoing series shot in a simple yet compelling way, we could move people in increments. This made sense because I believe being thoughtful about Content in the Ecosystem makes it easier to move people through the Matrix of Engagement.

Being thoughtful in this case meant shooting for 4,000 views across platforms with about 1,000 people getting to the end. Because if we can incrementally move 1,000 people at a time to be committed to the organization's systemic theory of change, we have the ability get a real impact in action, support, and fundraising.

Methods for Generating Views

With audience and intended impact laid out, you can now focus on how you are going to get the views. This is the crucial piece for making the impact you want with video. Think through the channels you have and what the views might be worth for you.

Here is a breakdown of the different channels, their value, and effort.

SOCIAL MEDIA

Social media channels and algorithms currently thrive on video. In this space, it is a question of how much video you can feed it. However, if you don't have active social media channels, you can't bank much here. Take a look at engagement you've had around other content and try to approximate the amount of engagement you might have in the future. Good video often performs as well or better than great images on Facebook and Twitter. Instagram can be a bit harder to gauge image vs. video. Also consider longevity: does the video have a short shelf life, meaning it is only relevant for a few days, for a few weeks, or is it evergreen?

If it is relevant over a longer period of time, you should have a plan that lays out when you'll be posting it over time. If it is a short period, really focus in on your optimal time slots. And if the views are critical, even consider an extra post or two beyond your normal good rate. Meaning, if you normally get 2,000 views on a post and you think posting this video a third time will bring your average down to 400 views, it might be worth it if you have a goal focused on shifting outcomes.

EMAIL

Email and video planning can be tricky. If it's a big video with important production value, it makes sense to email but to what impact? Is your email audience your target audience? If not, you should decide if your email list impacts your target audience by sharing it with them or helping raise public discourse around the video.

Two ways to think of measuring the impact on your target audience are in terms of viewer and number of views. Being a viewer is simple—you need to get your target audience's eyeballs on the video. Number of views is another soft form of impact. Let's

IMPACT

"Video can engage and drive real impact. But always know if your supporters are the audiences to be impacted or to help drive impact."

say you have a political or corporate target that you think can be influenced by knowing your video got a lot of views. In this case, it might not be about exact quality of views, but total number of views plus getting to your target.

Good email list segmentation and tagging are important because they help you target your content to the right audience. Consider whether you'd like to generate a view or a share. I know it might seem intuitive that if people watch the video, they will share it, but just think about how many videos you see that you don't share. People are more likely to share a video when asked. Deciding which is more important will help you make the right ask to the right audience to watch or to share. You may have different segments from your list with which you can target different calls to action. Perhaps one group you want to target for watching and one for sharing. That's ideal, because it means you are making very intentional decision on audience types and the impacts you want.

Lastly on email, know what it is worth for you to get views. As in, what level of email unsubscribes are you willing to withstand for sending the video? It is a question you should ask on all emails. Paid email acquisition rates average $1-5 per email address for most political and nonprofits. Then consider that the statistics that come from M+R every year show most nonprofits average $1-10 per email. What could your costs in unsubscribes be if you are reaching the wrong audience on your email list? It's good to know your cost per email address for your organization and balance that with getting views via organic or paid social media promotion.

WEBSITE

Many people imagine that, when they put a video on their site, people will just come watch. Well if you look at many organizations' youtube stats on videos on pages, you'll probably see they are low. The reality for organizations for whom media isn't their main focus, means the website is rarely the consumption point of video viewing unless driven there by email, social, press, or ads.

I think you should put all relevant videos on your site, just don't expect a lot of views to just happen on the site. The views you get there are more likely to be of high organizational value. Someone coming to your site and engaging in a lot of content builds a higher likelihood for long-term engagement.

ONLINE ADS

Here is where getting the audience you want is truly up to you and your budget. Knowing your intended audience on a granular level can have huge impact. You can refine by many key factors, even making sure people on your email list see it. Make sure you know what you are doing or work with an ads consultant before you just "boost" the video to get a lot of random views.

PARTNERS AND CELEBRITIES

How are you thinking about engaging partners to ask them to share it? Is it a good email ask for them? Would it make an easy ask for social media?

Same for celebrities or people that carry some social clout in the audience you want to reach.

EARNED MEDIA

Creating a video that has a press-worthy angle should be thoughtful. Why is it press-worthy? Are you exposing something new? Expressing a new angle? You should be able to think through what kind of success you've had before with press and determine to what level you think there may be additive views. Maybe not just from broadcast or online media, but also niche online publications and blogs.

Video Planning: Production Tips

If you haven't spent a lot of time in video, here are a few tips to help you make a video more productive and your work with a video firm much easier.

#1 CREATE A SCRIPT OR OUTLINE

Make sure you have a basic working script and at least an outline of how the shots will work together. What are the things you need to have said and imagery you need?

#2 SHOOT ONLY WHAT YOU NEED

This is very informed by #1. Often folks think I will just shoot some stuff and we'll edit it down. I personally worked as a freelance videographer for about a year. The biggest early mistake I made was shooting too much. Why would I want to review four hours of video to cut down to a few minutes?

#3 KEEP IT SIMPLE

Keep it truly simple, simple. Are you making a quick DTC (Direct to Camera) from a supporter or staffer? Don't try to add in a bunch of funky cuts and edits. Just keep it to the core content. And even on the longer pieces, don't rely on a lot of fancy cuts and text moving. Only caveat there being, if you are doing a full video or full sections of motion graphics or animations.

#4 LIVE EVENTS ARE HARD

Whether you are hoping to get shots from a live event or cover something live, remember it's hard to get the exact or compelling shots. Make a shot list. This goes back to have a script or outline. That should help you be in position to get the right shots at the right time.

Going truly live is a different beast. My best recommendation is either be ready for something very unscripted or have your viewers wait through some awkwardness. I've personally had very mixed results and, to date, have yet to have an experience where I would say going live was better than having at least a few seconds to a few minutes to share great clips on social.

While on the Obama campaign, we experimented with live using the Google+ YouTube Live tool. A campaign surrogate went very, very off message while we were live. Needless to say that was the last impromptu live stream I suggested for the cycle.

#5 AUDIO

From tips above, audio is so crucial. Make sure you plan to have that good audio. How will you get the sounds you need? Editing audio without expensive high-quality software and equipment is rarely easy.

#6 LIGHTING AND BACKGROUND

Take some time and plan where you will shoot. Especially if you are planning to do something simple in an office. Can you declutter the background? Then make sure the lighting will work. Make sure there isn't some awkward overhead or side lighting you can't control.

Summary

Strategic video means planning for view-based goals and for how video can impact other goals. Having a video launch plan specific to the platform of distribution will increase the likelihood of engagement. As always, know your goals, and be prepared to pay for high-quality video, or review our tips for making sure you produce your own work well. Audio and lighting are film basics, so make sure you give consideration to the quality of both.

Stories and Studies

Presented by Liz Rubin, Josh Burstein, Katrina Mendoza, and Jeff Gabriel.

Using Comprehensive Event Coverage to Energize Ecosystems of Content

LIZ RUBIN // Founder, CEO and Eco-Filmpreneur, *ECODEO* // www.lizrubindp.com

When Ecodeo has been hired to capture events, our team produces carefully researched content that includes key players, thematic experts, and tries to cover the diversity, versatility and widest range of perspectives at the event. As a team hired to capture the "moment" or "essence" of the dialogues at these conferences and events, our end goal with the delivered video package is that it should serve as an invaluable media tool for the clients/partners that hired us. If the videos expand the dialogues online across wide audiences after the actual event and bring new folks into the dialogues, that extends the value potentially for months or years to come.

In 2016, The (IUCN) International Union for the Conservation of Nature asked us to make a film documenting the incredible IUCN World Conservation Congress, 2016. Since its start as the IUCN General Assembly in 1948, the IUCN World Conservation Congress has grown in scope and prominence to become the largest and most democratic recurring conservation event in the world. A United Nations Sustainable Development meeting that takes places once every four years, the IUCN Congress brings top scientists and academics together with world leaders and decision-makers from governments, civil society, indigenous communities, and business. Together, they share the latest in conservation science, launch new initiatives, and decide on actions to address pressing conservation and sustainable development challenges. The knowledge shared and the decisions made over those 10 days helps define our shared path to a sustainable future and move historic global climate and sustainable development agreements into action.

Ecodeo had a 10-person crew on the ground covering this enormous event. We conducted 35 interviews, filmed hundreds of sessions, and interviewed climate heroes and UN delegates and ambassadors such as Jane Goodall and E.O. Wilson, UNFCCC's Christina Espinoza, Antonio Benjamin, Inger Anderson.

Although we produced a targeted five-minute main video in English with subtitled versions in French and Spanish to inspire participants, highlight outcomes, and show the Congress's global relevance and significance, much of the photographic and documentary video content we captured was designed to be used in communications after the event and in the lead-up to the 2020 Congress, as well as on social media platforms. We also produced six designed and thematic videos focused on different aspects of sustainable development. In the end, Ecodeo delivered a substantial content package for IUCN to use as a comprehensive media and communications tool over the next few years, helping to keep critical conservation narratives activated within their vast global networks.

The Digital "Run n' Gun" of Video Production

**JOSH BURSTEIN // Senior Creative Advisor, *The Democrats* //
www.joshburstein.com**

To produce good political communications, you have to be versed at capturing digital content in real-time.

Problem: You rarely have the luxury of time and resources with anything on a campaign. Now, more than ever, one emotional video, motivating NowThisian clip or candid photo has mileage well beyond a single social post. You're buried in meetings and other responsibilities and have to physically show up to generate these assets. This is an intensive process, but even if you're not "The Video Guy," there are ways to be reactive, improvisational, and seek quality in what you create on the ground.

During the 2012 race, I was in Green Bay, WI, when we found out Paul Ryan was going to be the VP candidate. Surprise quickly turned to anger: we spent weeks navigating approval chains to produce (the next morning) a highly curated, Wisconsin-specific, rally cry of a GOTV video. The Field team had gone to great lengths to find us an ideal location and the absolute best "Real People" to feature. I called in favors with every local filmmaker I could find to do this one right. The timing of this news meant we needed to scrap the whole concept and move priorities to Rapid Response. After all, Wisconsinites know Paul Ryan best.

And that's when it clicked: we didn't burden the field for nothing. We just brought a dozen volunteers—teachers, doctors, steelworkers—to the most scenic farm in rural Wisconsin for a rapid response video. I tore up the script (the same script I had considered my baby the day before) to interview each person on what "Wisconsin Knows" about Paul Ryan, and turned around a nationally viable video in short order. We grabbed photos and quotes for additional content. This was a great day.

If you're trying to capture authentic content, authentically, your plans often get blown up. This is true whether you're on the ground highlighting organizers, shadowing candidates, covering rallies—the best preparation is to continually put yourself at the intersection of opportunity and chance. Show up. Do it live!

Have the right, lean gear always close at hand. You should be able to weave through a crowd or hop in the back of a truck with your filming equipment. For all other instances, trick out your iPhone with a decent microphone and extend its battery life. Embolden an artistic and competent intern with a DSLR camera for when you inevitably need to be in three places at once.

Continually redefine your own success. Don't go out with only one pathway to achieving your goal, or you will often be disappointed. Too many factors are out of your control, make chaos comfortable and deputize volunteers you can trust for UGC. Quickly review everything that was captured, not just for what was intended—you may mine some gems, especially when folks think the camera isn't focused on them.

Get close. The best shots happen in the moments between events—humanity and humbleness backstage, one-on-one conversations. To emphasize: your unique advantage is access—proximity to candidates and organizers, and their comfort with you. You also have a leg up on every journalist because your team alone often knows where the story may break next—nothing is stopping you from commanding a news cycle with quality, timely content.

A Crash Course in Powerful Video Production

KATRINA MENDOZA // CEO, *Ditch The Box Studios /*
k.alexandramendoza@gmail.com

Good content is strategic, and great content takes time. As an activist, organizer, and business owner the urgency of asks can mean walking a thin line between the two. I've often asked, how do I make a powerful, high quality video on a budget with a short timeline? The most straightforward answer I've found:

Tell an engaging story.

As a communicator and video producer, I know that emotional appeal is the number one way to engage attention, and the best way to create emotion is with storytelling. My wife and I have made a living producing small budget videos for growing community groups, and we didn't need fancy equipment to do it. If you can tell a story, then the tech will stand on its own, but if your story is weak, then the tech quality won't necessarily matter (especially if your video is web-based). Emphasize the story!

Here's my quick list to capture and produce an engaging story for videos with (or without) interviews.

When filming interviews...

1. Cut the script. As a video editor, the bane of my existence is a rehearsed answer on camera. No matter what words are being said, if there's no emotion behind it, then it strips the video of feeling. For this reason, I typically don't prep my interviewees, and as I'm filming, I'm receptive to the emotional tidbits. It's ok to prep your questions for yourself just to make sure you touch on all of them. Scripts are powerful if you can write a script for a confident interviewee, and the writing feels powerful when you read it.

2. Ease in and draw out. Since the goal is to capture emotion, I use the first two minutes of the interview to get the person speaking on camera to relax and release. This can be easy or hard depending on the person. Then when I feel they're ready, I offer my questions, which are focused on drawing out the most emotional and relevant info. Questions that help me achieve this include turning points, big wins, realizations, preferences and values, decision-making, those life moments that feel defining in one way or another.

3. Focus on the big picture. At the point that you're interviewing someone, you should have a sense of why you want the video in the first place. It's important to keep this in mind so you can ensure you capture the interview bits you want to use in the video.

While editing interviews...

1. Highlight the most positive perspectives. I will cut out any negatively-focused sound bites as I'm editing, and this simple filter really elevates the story of the video. We're so surrounded by negative news and stories, that simply having a positive perspective feels fresh and powerful. To identify negative and positive bites, simply ask if what they say feels heavy/dark (negative) or uplifting and light (positive).

2. Let the story unfold. I usually jump into projects ready for the content to speak to me. In other words, I take the best of what I've got and, by the time I've gathered my selects, the story has usually appeared and formed in my mind.

Editing beyond (or without) interviews...

1. Music is everything. As a universal language of emotions, music is the key to setting the tone for your video piece. It can create a story without words and it can destroy a great story by misrepresenting the tone. Decide what emotion the video (or part of the video) needs, then look for the music by thinking about the styles, instruments, and pacing that may fit. Be patient. Finding the right song can be the turning point for a piece. I often splice up multiple songs for a single video because the tone will change from scene to scene, just be careful about mixing music so it feels like a smooth transition. Original composition is the best if you know someone who can help, or if you have the resources for it. Otherwise, audioblocks have been a great, affordable resource. Here's a referral code for a discount: http://bit.ly/audio4me

2. Choose the B roll that adds color to the story. B roll is the term for media that supports the main content (i.e., interview footage). In a timeline, it's the photos and videos you stack on top of your interview footage. For videos like events, I will sometimes have no interview footage or voice over audio, and the entire film will stand on its own with music and b roll. In these cases, think of your music as your main story, with the visuals helping to write the story. Choosing good B roll is a matter of contrast and perspective. I like to Google search for past content, historical footage, and I always ask clients for access to any and all media they have. I'll even take screenshots of websites or images when necessary. There are also some great tools online for downloading videos from

YouTube and Facebook, but you'll want to watch out for copyright rules. There are many sites online with royalty-free footage, just search for creative commons, archive.org, Democracy Now, etc. An affordable alternative for great content is videoblocks. Here's a referral code for a discount: http://bit.ly/video-me

The last tip for powerful video: start with the big picture and purpose for your video, and then drill down into the details. The more specifically intentional your content is, the more powerful it will be. Happy shooting and easy editing!

SOCIAL MEDIA

Where to even start? Most advice I've seen is wrong on a platform by platform basis, because the advice is almost absent of connecting it to goals and impact. I guess let's start with, it is not free. At the very least it takes an investment in staff time and that is a cost. Done well and at scale, social media can be fairly expensive and yet there has never been a better way to have consistent engagement with supporters than social media.

How to use this chapter

Non-Digital Leadership or Management: Hopefully you already understand the power of social media. You should read this chapter to understand real strategy better.

Digital/Tech Staffers: Practical knowledge for you to create truly strategic plans, create plans that drive real engagement, and leverage the most of this resource.

New Staff/Activists: Social media can be a powerful way to build exposure for a new organization, campaign, or project. It is one of the tools that can be leveraged with a minimal budget but with the capacity to manage.

KEY TAKEAWAYS AND ELEMENTS:
- Strategic thoughts on how to think about different mediums and platforms
- Strategic thinking for a specific organization and campaign sizes
  - Small and Abstract, or Small and Local

- Moderately sized organizations or political campaigns
- Statewide organizations or political campaigns
- National organizations
- Deeper strategy for various platforms, and introductions to deep theory with "The Ecosystem of Content" and "The Matrix of Engagement"
- Planning guidelines to help you publish, engage, analyze, and do more

The Matrix of Engagement, similar to the ladder of engagement, is about how you make a proactive ask and manage supporters. If the Matrix of Engagement is how you think about the ask and engagement of supporters, then the companion theory to that would be an Ecosystem of Content. Basically, everything you use to engage users is content. Tweets, meta tags, subject lines, videos, URL names, Facebook descriptions, are all kinds of content. Social media is one of the most rapid and evolving spaces for real-time, content-based engagement.

There is no one-size-fits-all social media plan or growth plan. I firmly believe anyone that tries to tell you that is a hack. Just like every section of the book, the main question here is, what is your goal? Social media is not one thing. Social media is a series of different content platforms. You need to start there with your thinking because each social media channel is a platform with different functions and abilities. The nuance of digital involves a bunch of interrelated platforms and mediums for content. Each medium and content platform functions differently, and I'm going to break this down for clarity on utilizing each one well.

MEDIUMS AND PLATFORMS

Mediums are the pieces of content, like written articles (on another site or your blog), images, gifs, videos, short text messages (could be in SMS, Tweet, Facebook), emails, and web content that is a page or combination of words plus image or video on a page of another site.

Platforms are the ways in which content and actions are presented. Platforms include everything from your site, Facebook, Twitter, Tumblr, Petition sites, fundraising sites, Pinterest, SnapChat, SMS, and platforms to send email and host petitions connected to your site.

So here is the conundrum: Facebook, Tumblr, SnapChat, Instagram, Pinterest, You-Tube, Google+, Reddit (kind of social), MySpace (still exists somehow) are all between fairly and very different social media platforms. And there are more with reasonable and niche followings. You would want a different content and engagement strategy for each. So how do you choose?

It's goal time. Is your goal to inspire action? Are you seeking to build a broader audience to engage around your issue? Do you want to use social media to build buzz for events? Recruit new people? Get more event attendees?

A good top-level place to start is thinking about how you are going to function as an organization, with the goals of the organization, and the resources you have.

Real Life Example: Obama 2012 and Google+

During the 2012 election cycle, Google+ was just coming out. I thought it could be a game changer if it opened up a new platform for engagement. Joe Rospars and Teddy Goff, being the long-seasoned Senior Digital Strategists that they are, cautioned any optimism until we could see the audience and how it would really work. In 2008, a few people were constantly talking about Twitter, but couldn't answer how it could amount to votes. So as a platform, it didn't align with the campaign goals at the time. Then in 2012, it had matured as an online platform that was excellent at a rapid response, building online conversation, and could be converted into actions like attending events. An intern at the time Danielle Butterfield- who now is quite a digital ads strategist—did some research and we made suggestions on how it could be used. It was piloted but ultimately the resources were pulled back, because even an organization that large had finite resources and one goal. That goal was to get Barack Obama to 270 electoral votes, and anything that couldn't be benchmarked as adding to volunteers, dollars, or votes, wasn't worth the expense of money or human power. What are your 270 electoral votes? Is it winning an election, getting an initiative passed, protecting a river, defending human rights across the globe...? Whatever your goal is, you need to make critical decisions and answer if a platform is helping you meet that goal or drawing down resources.

Social Media, Catered to You

Here are a few real-world examples of looking at different platforms based on size and scale. I'll give a few tips further on how to think about different platforms in the Ecosystem of Content.

YOU'RE SMALL AND ABSTRACT

I spent some time six months ago talking to a partner foundation. They were getting pressure from the board to be better on social. We chatted for a bit so I could understand their goals. They didn't have an inherently large audience or a large base of donors. Funds came from large donors and not a large group of small donors, so their goal for social media was to offer a connection for those looking, and to alleviate the board's concern they weren't doing enough. Since their mission was to give grants and not spread messaging, I stayed focused on that advice.

I said you should do Facebook because it is expected. With the resources you have, I would just post grants and articles about grants. For sure, post some albums from events. It's enough to make the board satisfied, and enough content for those funders and people associated with the organization to find some content with which to connect. Since messaging isn't your mission, I don't think you'll ever have enough content to build much of a following on Twitter, so it's a bit of a take it or leave it. If you do it, try to post every other day or so. And I would recommend nothing for other platforms. By knowing goals, you can think about what the platforms are good at and if they're leverage-able for your project.

YOU'RE SMALL AND LOCAL

Different scenario—if you're working on a small local initiative or project, social media might be your best friend. Facebook can be very powerful for local organizing. If your goal is to connect with and organize people in a local community and their neighbors, it can go a long way. In most local campaigns, your goals would involve messaging, recruitment, events, and possibly turnout if it is an item to vote on.

FEEDBACK

"Does the work and time you put in actually move the needles on your work or does it just feel like it does?

Make sure you have goals so you can measure feedback."

Facebook could work great here using its Groups and Page features. Groups empower neighbors to engage and invite each other in, organizing local events together, thus allowing you to build action by making it clear that neighbors are supporting the campaign. Using a page and being small and local might make it hard to get the traction you need for Facebook to show your content in people's timelines. This is one reason groups are effective for local organizing because updates show up in your notifications. If you are going to set up a page, know that it might not get the consistent engagement you'd expect because of other pages and personal content muscling your page out of people's timelines. It might be worth exploring small boosts of even $25 targeted to locals you want to reach for engagement when needed.

There is an old saying in political campaigns that yard signs don't vote. This is true for major elections where all candidates have name recognition. But it isn't true when the name or issue recognition is low. The signs can't vote, but it is valuable as a part of issue persuasion or education. To see someone you respect the opinion of getting behind an issue validates it. This is very true online where we become peer-to-peer validators.

Would you use invest in Twitter? That's a good question. Do a number of your staffers or key volunteers really know Twitter and massaging? Would they have a strategy for finding locals to follow and engage with? Could you draft a strategy around that content leading to engagement? I do think it's okay for small campaigns and projects to let qualified volunteers help run online social. This isn't an endorsement of giving the keys to interns, but do you have someone that understands a platform well enough to engage in a strategy for the platform? If not, they probably shouldn't be driving it. The potential for harm is possibly greater than the return.

How do you know if you should use Instagram or SnapChat or YouTube? Again, it's about the goals. Are you trying to engage younger community members not using Facebook? (Although, it is a bit of a myth Facebook still has a reasonably high saturation rate among all age ranges). Do you know for sure they aren't there? If yes, do you have someone that understands how to use the platform? Not all platforms work well for engagement. If you are sharing messages from peer-to-peer, maybe SnapChat will work. If it's about protecting something beautiful or building something, the imagery of Instagram or Pinterest might have use there. But the question should be: is going shallow in a few places better than deep on one of the bigger networks like Facebook and Twitter?

If you're a political campaign, say yes to both Facebook and Twitter. You need to give people something to connect to, and if you want to be in office, you should be building a Twitter account to engage with constituents.

MODERATELY SIZED EXAMPLES

So what if you are at a moderate to a medium-sized organization or campaign, maybe something with 10 to 20 people? At this point, you should have at least one, if not two to three people, involved in the digital realm. Social media is an element you should be considering in a real way, and you should put real consideration into how you want to maximize it. Let's split here a bit between electoral and NGO.

If you are an NGO, you're probably in this size, and you probably have either a service to deliver or an issue to make a change. How do you engage with people in your mission? That is a crucial question to finding your goal. The way you interact is relatively different if you are a service provider, an organization that needs people to drive messaging, or one that encourages local issue organizing. Part of asking these questions is identifying

ENGAGE

"Make sure your social strategy is focused around engaging your supporters on a deeper level and finding a balance that creates an opening for new supporters."

your audience. If you are a service provider, your key audience should be figuring out how you can use social media to connect with those that might need your services and those that support your mission and want to help by volunteering or funding it. The question you should be able to answer long run is: are you engaging with those audiences?

This is a time to make a choice because you need to think about who is likely to be the core audience of your content. Is your audience who you serve, who you empower, or who you mobilize? Pick your primary focus and develop content for them. It is okay to work material for different audiences, but with each piece, you should know which audience you intend to connect with. It is the social media equivalent of the right ask, right audience, right time.

Regardless of which way you go, I am going to suggest you be Facebook forward. It is still the largest, most robust social media platform. At this size, you should be planning on at least a piece of content daily. And think about how you could use it to connect new people to your organization. Will you drive the services you promote, possibly with a modest ad budget? Will you use events to ask supporters to invite in new people to your issue or cause? If you don't have experienced design folks on staff, I recommend hiring a graphic designer to make you a few templates you can update. Quality looking images go a long way in terms of reach and engagement.

Twitter is going to be a question of how you could and should use it. It can be a good place to find some people looking for services or volunteering. If recruitment like this is important, try the more advanced search features. At the very least, use it to drive updates about your organization. And having an account makes it possible for active users to link people to your organization. Planning should be about what the primary focus is going to be. Is it engagement, messaging, or just updates? If it is to drive messaging or engagement, make sure you are investing enough time and energy, so you impact the goals you want.

Other platforms are in the same boat as above. Does your mission lend itself to one of the niche platforms? Are you gaining strategically by diverting resources here?

ELECTORAL MODERATELY SIZED EXAMPLES

In modern politics, you should have a social media strategy that is about messaging, connection, and engagement. These are three different, but interwoven, ways to use social media in an Ecosystem of Content.

You should have clear messaging filters through which your content is channeled. It should drive the words used and images selected. It should match up to your campaign's message and feel. If you're all business, it should have that look and feel and consistent message. If you are all about the local community, your imagery and design should match up with that.

Because you are a political campaign, you should think about connecting in a different way. What are the issues and characteristics you want to connect to the electorate with? You should be able to answer that, and plan content around it. Content created on a whim will only get you so far, and once in awhile, it might do very well, but possibly for the wrong reasons. Crafting good content builds a connection between the candidate and their constituents. It should be built around shared values and issues. Keep it real—people can spot fakeness on social media almost as much as in-person.

Take the message and connection you are building and translate it into engagement. Engagement on issues. Engagement on civic participation like registering to vote and getting others registered. And make sure to make asks to engage in the campaign. Ask people to get involved, tell them how they can do it, and respond when they show support or have questions. Have staff also positively engage supporters in comments and Twitter conversations.

Facebook should be a well-balanced mix of video messaging, issue content that is a mix of articles links and images, shareable images, and campaign events people can invite others to. At this level, you should have a social media editorial calendar that you use to plan messaging and event building.

Twitter should also be a given. You should be using it to share campaigns messages. Show the candidate's personality and engage with supporters. I personally recommend also following folks in the community in which the candidate is running. There are pros and cons to this, but I recommend a blanket strategy where you find very local accounts and try to proactively follow people you can identify, whatever the electoral district is.

You should have a youtube channel at this level. You can drive people there and ask them to engage and share content. Keep an eye on what content is loaded with your campaign videos. Try to develop some content specifically to match up with what people might search about your campaign.

You should be thinking about the Ecosystem of Content. Can you design a suite of images on an issue that works well for Facebook and Twitter? Are you developing petitions or issue blogs on your website that work well for social sharing? Are you creating issue related petitions that recruit supporters from Twitter and Facebook to your email list?

Instagram, SnapChat, and other social media platforms are really going to be a balanced call again. You need to know what your in-depth strategy is. Is it worth going deeper to create more thoughtful content for other social media platforms? Whatever you do, don't hesitantly start a channel and stop. Would you want to elect someone who initiates a project and doesn't have a plan to finish it? Nope, you want to engage with an organization that has clear goals and a path to get there. Be that organization.

ORGANIZATIONAL SCALE NGO

What if you are at an organization or campaign, maybe with 20 to 50 people? I will stop here as well because I am roughly assuming once you fall into the 50 plus person size, you often have the budget to afford the consultants needed. This book as a goal is meant to serve folks that are in small to medium-sized organizations to bolster support for their digital planning.

At a 20 to 50 person organization doing some kind of campaigning, I am hoping you have at least four to five people working on aspects of digital campaigning. In the staffing section too, we should be at a place where more staff are rolling digital into their role and thinking about how what they do translates to the internet.

Social media at this size should be very thoughtful. The Ecosystem of Content should be a thoughtful mix that drives your mission and works for each platform. Facebook is still an under-tapped resource for most organizations. Do you have an interplay between site content, Facebook posts, and email?

A way to think about this is to consider whether or not you're developing good content that is shareable and readable from Facebook. Are you tracking the engagement from the post back to the goal of the content? Is it an expanded reach of a conversion or conversion on a sign-up? Are you also developing content that will work well for sharing? Are you building your email channel from Facebook engagement? Do you then send emails to re-engage people with your page and to spread your organization's messaging, broadening the reach again and reactivating folks? You should be able to take your mission and benchmark engagement that drives your organization to that mission.

Facebook is not a novelty, but a way to drive and build engagement. You should have a serious plan on how communications and two-way engagement happen. If you want to follow good best practices with content types, the frequency of your posts should be at least three times a day, and not so close together that your content competes against itself. You will really start to see what resonates with your Facebook community. Now, don't only feed the community what it likes. Find the balance between the easy and shareable content with the deeper content you really want people to spend time with.

At this size, you should certainly be thinking about some online ads budgets for Facebook content. I'm personally not a fan of buying page likes because I think your content and an interplay with email should get you there. But I know firsthand when used well, it is an excellent platform for email list building and content engagement ads.

Twitter at this size is a must, and you can take the elements above and expand. I was asked a while back, what I would do differently if I were at a large political campaign again. The answer is, to have a role called "Architect of Story." Someone who structures how content rolls out from which voices online. Twitter is a perfect platform for this. If you are launching a new campaign, are there different points of view that different members of your organization would tackle it from? If so, could you think about how their voices play

EXECUTE

"At this size of an organization, your social media should not be haphazard. Experiments are great, that's different. Make sure your execution is tight."

out and interact with each other on Twitter? Would one account tweet more about only the facts, another about the human connection, and another on how to take action? Could you have them retweet and interact with each other in an authentic way? Think about it as a place where people can interact with one another in a public and organized way.

UNSCRIPTED TWITTER REALITY

During the 2012 Obama campaign, I found myself in North Carolina meeting with an active Twitter user who I followed because I followed supporters in many states. They told me they appreciated the real interaction between the HQ staff, naming people they were following such as Mitch Stewart, Jeremy Bird, Yohannes Abraham, Betsy Hoover, and myself on Twitter. We would often tweet sports related jabs, retweet each other, and share snippets of in-person conversations. This volunteer appreciated that it humanized us beyond people they just got emails from. It made us real people beyond email sender names, and it deepened that supporter's engagement with the campaign.

So what would it look like if you intentionally invested in building out good content for staff accounts and encouraged a real cross handle engagement?

Tweets don't just go into the wind. They are the easiest piece of social content to track. I would encourage you to invest in a tracking system and look at what kind of message reach and conversion on goals you are getting. But please don't look at numbers for two months and say it doesn't work. Use benchmarks to figure out what does and doesn't work for you.

YouTube should also be used at this scale. I would encourage you to ask the question, what might someone search related to our campaign? Can we create a video that answers that search? How would we build a channel that is engaging, and maximizes the robust community on YouTube?

And we find ourselves at the question of whether or not to invest in Instagram, Snap-Chat, Pinterest, Tumblr, and other platforms. Again, this should be a real investigation into how it would impact your organization. At RAN, we had an Instagram account and built it as a second tier platform. Because we still had a lot more depth that we could achieve on Facebook and Twitter, it didn't make sense to invest in Instagram. The theory was simple: let's push simple content on Instagram that was previously created for Facebook. If it grows, that's great, but since we can't do link conversion from there, it would make more sense to invest in places where we could do conversion. If you have the luxury of a well-known organizational brand and you want to use Instagram to reinforce brand campaigns and engagement, I think that's a great goal. But make sure you've got a plan that establishes benchmarks that make it clear what you're hoping to get from the channel.

ORGANIZATIONAL SCALE STATEWIDE ELECTORAL

This section is similar to what was discussed in the previous section for a moderately sized campaign. I would again raise real caution from going shallow into several platforms.

Instead, I would think about what it looks like to have a very deep strategy in Face-book and Twitter. Be sure to use Facebook to really community build. Make it easy to connect to your campaign on Facebook and find ways to engage. Think about Facebook as essential to your messaging and community building strategies. Put yourself in the role of supporter and develop content that moves them through the Matrix of Engage-ment. Don't make it an afterthought, you want to be developing thoughtful Facebook first videos. Think through how this platform is essential in an Ecosystem of Content, moving people to your site, to email list, and back from those places to engage on Face-book. Often overlooked is the soft entrance of Facebook events. It can feel less daunting to sign-up for an event on Facebook with a new organization than a formal web form, but make sure you have a good strategy to go from your Facebook event to a database.

A good strategy should include running smart Facebook ads reaching for your target demographics for volunteering, registration, and turnout. Whatever it is, ads help you reach the core audience you are investing energy in reaching to begin with.

If you are planning to have an impact over these channels then you should be investing in training staff and volunteers on how to use Facebook and Twitter to reach campaign goals. What would such a plan look like for you? Ensure you have a good way to make it easy for supporters to share messaging and recruit others.

Here are a few deeper level considerations to get you thinking strategically:

EXECUTE

"If you are serious about your campaign, a volunteer should NOT be managing your execution of social media. They can offer support, but should not be your core management."

- Imagine you have someone from digital or communications take in a role like an "Architect of Story" mentioned in the NGO section above.
- Think through how content could move and be promoted by all the staff in the organization.
- Work on the possibility of you empowering organizers to be amplifiers.
- Tell the story of the work such as sharing images of organizers connecting the community from their accounts, and amplified by communications staff and candidates.
- Plan out organizers connecting with volunteers over social and working together to amplify core campaign messaging.

It is all about making sure your plan fits both the size of your organization and the goals you are trying to impact. Make conscious decisions about which platforms you are going to invest in with staff time and resources.

Platforms, The Ecosystem of Content, and The Matrix of Engagement

I want to be sure the underlying advice of planning doesn't get lost in any of the individual sections above.

You need to have a plan that takes into account that each social media platform is different. That plan also needs to be cognizant of a complete Ecosystem of Content.

An Ecosystem of Content is everything you use to engage users. Tweets, meta tags, subject lines, videos, URL names, and Facebook descriptions are all kinds of content. Social media is one of the most rapidly evolving spaces for real-time, content-based engagement.

Content should be purposefully created for the goal you want to reach and the platform it's on. This means creating sign-ups and petitions that convert well from social media. URLs that are descriptive can be read on social before someone even clicks. Were you thinking about meta-images and content on the page for organic social media shares?

Is there interplay between Twitter, Facebook, email, site informational content, blog, and actions? Do you think about a new item going out across the ecosystem at large and which piece drives which?

Given that you have mission-driven goals, how are you thinking about a Matrix of Engagement and how does it play out on social? Think about ways to get to the right ask, to the right audience, at the right time. This isn't all about rapid response. It's about using social data, social recruiting, and driving message. Is the right ask to join a conversation on Twitter or push a new video on Facebook or YouTube? Is the right ask to make an email ask to use social for peer donations?

It's about time, planning, and action. If you are just getting started, don't let planning paralysis stop you. When I start working with a new group, we don't stop using social media until we have a plan. We look at where we are and discuss where we want to go.

Publish, Analyze and Publish

Don't be overly loose with social because major mistakes can set you back. The true beauty and curse of social media is volume. You have more space to experiment and test than most other spaces.

While Twitter and Facebook offer analytics in the platform, I highly recommend getting a more sophisticated all-in-one publishing and reporting system. That way you can set up performance and benchmarking reports.

FEEDBACK

"Social media is a feedback-rich environment. Make sure you have goals or are using data to develop goals."

Running a thoughtful system in Google analytics and conversion goals is going to take you to that next level. Conversion tracking, set up and used correctly, allows you to see what content, sent when, on which platform, converts to what you want. It only works when used consistently and properly, over weeks and months. When the right data is collected over time, it tells you some fascinating information about where to dig in more and what opportunities are growing.

Good analytics used with thoughtful benchmarks are a perfect compliment to creative content. It tells you where and when the content is connecting with audiences. It will be an ongoing cycle of publish and analyze and taking that information to draft new content to publish again.

Summary

Social media can seem like a beast, but if you think strategically according to mediums, platforms, and the specific size of your campaign/organization, you can simplify the process. Clarifying your strategy will allow you to dive more deeply into The Ecosystem of Content and The Matrix of Engagement (different frameworks for considering your contents' engagement). Remember to analyze what you publish, since good analytics with thoughtful benchmarks are the perfect complement to creative content.

Stories and Studies

Presented by Lisa Conn and Jordan Mandel.

Lessons on Community

LISA CONN // Civic Community Partnerships

My grandmother was an activist during the civil rights era in Virginia, and her bedtime stories left me obsessed with the power of ordinary people to scale change. Over the course of my career building movements for candidates (Janice Hahn '11, Barack Obama '12, Mike Bonin '13), advocating for causes (FWD.us), and building civic tools (Hustle, MIT Media Lab, Facebook), I've realized the hardest and most important part about civic engagement is figuring out how to scale in-person interactions and build collective action.

I spent three years as the National Organizing Director of FWD.us, where I led a team of organizers to engage the tech community in the fight for comprehensive immigration reform. I saw first hand how crucial it was to create and sustain engagement with community members, as well as the difficulty of scaling connection. Organizers would gain and lose people between events, and some volunteers would come one month, and then never again. It was a constant struggle.

I knew that if we could help connect community members to each other and engage in horizontal relationship building, we'd be able to grow and sustain a movement that wasn't entirely focused on the leader or the organizer. I saw the importance of the initial in-person meet-up, and the need for technology to help cultivate that relationship beyond just the event. Now that I'm at Facebook, working with civic community leaders every day, I see that Facebook Groups is the answer I was looking for.

For instance, through my role at Facebook, I helped a large civic foundation create a Facebook group in the lead up to their first convening summit. This group served to cultivate the community by creating connection opportunities for attendees so that they could establish a common bond and build relationships before the event. We hosted content within the group during the days of the event and made it the destination for all information. This made it incredibly easy to move community members from this one event to future events and sustained involvement with the organization. And most importantly, it helped people with shared interests and passions to better the world, to build meaningful relationships with each other. I have had dozens of follow up conversations with people I first connected within the group, met offline at the summit, and stayed in touch with through the Group. I know I'm not alone in this experience. That's community.

The New Media Landscape

**JORDAN MANDEL // Sr. Account Director—Midwest, *Spotify* //
http://bit.ly/2pFU8yD**

Over my 10 years in marketing, I've had a front-row seat for the rapid change that has swept across the digital landscape. These changes have dramatically impacted both the way consumers make purchase decisions and how marketers achieve their goals. I've worked on teams who have leveraged the proliferation of online data, technology, social media, and custom content to achieve goals ranging from electing President Barack Obama, to increasing market share for some of the world's largest brands.

While technology has made it easier than ever for consumers to engage with the content they love wherever and whenever they want—it has become more challenging than ever for brands to make strategy and purchasing decisions with their marketing budgets. Media agencies have felt this shift first hand, as declining attention spans create an incredible challenge in identifying the best times, places, and devices to reach consumers. Throw in workflow automation technology and online/offline measurement, and it's easy to see how this new age digital landscape can be overwhelming.

Ad agencies have been forced to evolve their approach to meet client demands for efficiency, transparency, and accountability. To keep up with the rate of change, agency execs have had to realign their resources to focus on automated buying strategies, data, and content creation. We must now consider that a marketer's video may be watched on a TV set at home, on a cell phone while commuting, or from a computer screen at the office. Digital buying strategies have largely split into two core buckets: automated/programmatic buying and digital content. With that, agency execs have embraced innovation and invested heavily in training and technology to ensure their teams are fully equipped to thrive into the future.

As buying continues to consolidate, the ad tech lumascape is beginning to contract. The shift in planning and buying strategies has brought tough times for smaller vendors and publishers due to the inability to offer significant ad inventory scale or efficiently priced content production. This has forced many vendors to be scrappy not just for media dollars, but simply getting on their clients' calendar. Meanwhile, the media conglomerates are capturing the lion's share of marketing dollars due to their ability to generate significant inventory scale through automated channels, to efficiently produce high-quality content, and oftentimes distribute the content they produce through their own content channels.

The shift will ultimately benefit brands by delivering the transparency and efficiency that the digital space has always lacked. Agencies have been pressured to keep up with the marketplace innovation through training and technology, preparing for the future and teaching their old dogs new tricks. All the while, vendors are quickly scrambling to stay in front of clients and keep up with the demands for innovation around automation, measurement, and creativity.

What a time!

SITE CONTENT, BLOGS, AND STORYTELLING

They aren't just words for words sake. Site content, written copy, blogs, and storytelling should all link to your theory of change and advance your goals in an intentional way. So the question will always be: how does this drive you to your goals?

Let's explore how strong planning behind site content (images, words, videos, etc.) that appear on your website will lead to the impact you want. We'll also dig into how a blog can serve many functions and how you can strategically think about the ways a blog can highlight your organization, your work, your theory of change, and meet goals. We'll tie it all together with a bigger theory on storytelling. Storytelling should be the bigger lens through which most content flows because story, not facts and explanation, is what moves people. But storytelling also takes more time and resources. Storytelling doesn't just move people to action once, it helps build deeper and more long-term engagement from supporters.

How to use this chapter

Non-Digital Leadership or Management: Your site content is important. Many organizations and campaigns have content inconsistencies across their website and it hurts the brand and engagement.

Digital/Tech Staffers: Good content is good strategy. Every word on your site matters. Content and copy have a direct correlation to SEO and engagement.

New Staff/Activists: Understanding content will help you grow in ways others aren't as proactive in. Use the practical guidance here as your starting place.

KEY TAKEAWAYS AND ELEMENTS:
- Strategy for thinking about key audiences like potential supporters and volunteers, current volunteers and supporters, media, and targets you want to influence
- Guidance for direct measurable impact, external measurable impact, anecdotal response, and increased engagement
- Strategic thinking for the right content and layout
- Strategic thinking for types of blogs and how to make implementation decisions
- Understanding the fundamentals of a story that place the reader as an ally, change agent, or connected to a narrative of Heroes and Villains

Site Content

You only invest in the content you have a clear plan for. Not just investing in paying outside support but in how you use current time resources. Well-planned content can lead to higher engagement around your issues, better conversions, and the impact you want. But you need to be intentional and be planning and iterating from creation to impact to promotion, and throughout review. That might sound like a lot, but simple tweaking should get you there. You can offer content in a very similar form to email. With email, we were focused on these three sections: Right Ask, Right Audience, Right Time. Site content is a bit more expansive and has some of the same formal elements albeit a little different.

For each piece of site content, you need to think about Right Audience, Right Impact, Right Content and Layout. Now, content might feel a little redundant, but I'm using that in this case as a catch-all, since it may refer to words, images, videos, embeds from social, or another type of media form.

Right Audience

Each section of the site should have an intended audience. This is who you intend to engage, convert, or sway. Now is the time to ask yourself, who do you actually want to impact or empower with the piece of content? Not every possible bucket of people, you should just pick one. Consistently I watch people in the issue and political space write content without having one key audience in mind. Often, folks will list three to four different audiences, and it typically misses the mark for every possible audience.

It is okay to have a secondary audience. A secondary audience should always be the 'nice to have seen the content' or the 'nice to have engaged.' That means, not the primary target. You should know what your intended impact is to the secondary audience as well. If your primary target is volunteers to engage with an issue, then maybe your secondary target might be a political or corporate institution you intend to move. While you aren't creating the content for the secondary target, what impact do you want them to feel if they see it?

IMPACT

"The right audience creates the impact you wanted from the content. If it doesn't, move into feedback and then brainstorm and plan again."

Here are a few ways to think about right audience and why it matters. Often people confuse a secondary target for their primary audience. Possible audiences could be potential supporters and volunteers, current volunteers and supporters, potential large funders, media, a target you are attempting to sway, or someone who knows and cares about a certain issue. There are certainly more audiences and probably dozens of subsets of each so you should go as deep as you like or keep it as top line as possible.

Here is a list of simple questions to ask yourself for some of these key audiences:

POTENTIAL SUPPORTERS AND VOLUNTEERS:

Does this content allow them to see themselves as a potential character in the content?
- This adds to relatability for the reader.

Is it clear how they can take action?
- This makes it clear for the reader how they can engage and for you it might be the goal you are trying to reach or a pathway to other engagement goals.

Is it clear what the problem and solution are?
- Problem without solution can feel overwhelming.

How do you make it clear that your action is a part of the solution?
- This raises the likelihood for engagement.

Is the content written in a way that is approachable and not overwhelming?
- Don't lose people by writing too narrowly or by being verbose.

CURRENT VOLUNTEERS AND SUPPORTERS:

How is this different from potential folks?
• Find ways to make it feel like it was written for people who are part of the tribe.

Are there phrases, organizational, or issue language that makes them feel like they are connected or on the inside of your project or issue?
• This helps bring that relatability even closer to the reader.

Have you shown how their work is part of the solution?
• So key in empowerment is showing the way for others.

Are there positive examples?
• These allow others to find what they want to model.

Did you intentionally choose to skip some introductory content?
• This will make it less applicable to new people but could make it feel more insidery.

MEDIA:

Is there something unique and reportable in what you produced?
• Make sure that stands out from top to bottom.

Are there clear quotes and highlights?
• Use good layout choices to make that pop.

Is the access to quality imagery or video accessible for their reproduction?
• Consider having that linked at the bottom as to not slow down page load times.

TARGET YOU ARE ATTEMPTING TO SWAY:

Is your ask to them clear in the content?
• Similar to media make it clear from top to bottom.

Does the content make your organization's or communities' power clear?
• This is your narrative be sure to own it.

Does your content care more about simplicity or the complex nuance of the issue?

- This is truly your choice and has to do with whether or not your target will resonate more with big simple call outs or if the in-depth, nuanced facts are important to them.

SOMEONE WHO KNOWS AND CARES ABOUT A CERTAIN ISSUE:

Have you thought properly about the depth and engagement they might be looking for?

How did you make intentional choices between the balance of some introductory information vs. getting into the weeds?

Is there a way to make a simplified introductory version to make the content more accessible?

What do you know about the audience to design the content for them?

Two Stories on Audience

While at Organizing for America, the Democratic/Obama organizing committee that existed from 2009-2011, we built out a fairly consistent system of volunteer-written content on volunteering. It was strongly advocating for Betsy Hoover, whose own belief in volunteerism and service was a core in the New Media (Digital) Organizing team. She helped lead a top-down belief in bottom-up organizing. From the beginning, we knew the target audience was current volunteers, with a secondary audience of potential volunteers. Why volunteer-produced content on volunteering written for other volunteers? That seems really meta.

First of all, it is an untold story outside of the final stretch of electoral campaigns. Yet, ongoing volunteering is critical to the health of the organization and mission. We had a well-known mantra of "Respect, Empower, Include." We knew that telling a story to this audience helped reforge these values we believed in because it was an organizing first organization and we believe featuring such stories truly respected the work on the ground. That it would also ensure that spotlighted volunteers would feel respected. Empowerment occurred in the drafting of content and resonated in the words in the blogs. Inclusion appeared in the content itself. We were making a conscious choice to elevate the story of volunteerism and community organizing to front pages and social media feeds consistently.

While we didn't have the capacity to track the day-to-day impact of the lifetime volunteerism of individuals spotlighted or to correlate volunteers who read it, the anecdotal data was still there. Volunteers who were spotlighted, often shared with staffers on many levels how appreciative they were of the opportunity to tell their stories. It made the volunteers who helped move the draft to publication feel more connected to each other and local staff. Feedback from volunteers who engaged with the localized volunteer stories, echoed similar appreciation even if they weren't the ones being spotlighted. Then other volunteers commented on how reading a piece of content made getting involved feel approachable. It became an important piece in the Ecosystem of Content that brought people into the organization and helped move them through what would be a full Matrix of Engagement.

Here is a different story about the right content presented to the right audience with shifting impact. Before I got to the Rainforest Action Network, the organization had worked on a major investment to connect the story of Conflict Palm Oil to the continued threat of the existence of orangutans. The audience was clear—they had narrowed down to moms in the U.S. as the main purchasers for children's snacks in the home. As they dug into their campaign against the Snack Food 20—targeting 20 of the worst corporate consumers of raw palm oil—it was a key audience to impact the shift of their corporate targets.

They built out great collateral and launched a video about Strawberry the orangutan. The video was a success earning media and hundreds of thousands of views. Content was connecting with their target audience, and an organization that had a track record with more radical activists was reaching what you would think of as typical everyday consumers of major snack brands. Folks signed online petitions and a few were willing to do some volunteering.

Then came higher level asks to take more action in their community. Join tactics like putting warning labels about conflict palm oil on products in stores. The action didn't happen. It was almost impossible to get the list of people they had recruited to take more radical action. At the end of the day, it was about the content the audience was designed for, being different from the new audience we needed.

In hindsight, it was easy to see that a second track of content designed for more radical activists willing to take more risks would have been ideal. That kind of content would have spotlighted that kind of action and encourage others to join. It was really about knowing what audience you need to engage or impact. To be clear, even though that original audience's engagement definitely shifted, a number of companies produced policies that lead to not purchasing Conflict Palm Oil, thereby protecting Indigenous communities, forests, and the endangered species living there. However, in the next phase when the companies were more dug in, a new audience and content created for that new audience was necessary.

Right Impact

By picking the right audience, you will be clearer on your intended impact. Sometimes it is getting a conversion on a fairly simple piece of site content like a donation page or petition. Other times, it is building engagement through readership of a blog or story or understanding the organizational theory of change. For each piece of content, you should be able to answer what the impact is. Not just impact, but how you will measure it. Measurement is key in knowing if you are lining up the work on the right content to the right audience to get the intended impact on your goals.

There are a number of ways to measure impact. Here are just a few.

DIRECT MEASURABLE IMPACT

These are the impacts that are easy to measure like sign-up for an event. Sign a petition. Donate. Complete any number of discrete and trackable actions that you can assign a goal to.

EXTERNAL MEASURABLE IMPACT

There are a number of ways to measure external impact. Earned media around the content is a validation by the press that your information or design of information has broader relevance. A way to measure it is how many stories or articles you are looking for post-production. Another measurement could be getting partners to share and link to the content as validation. It means they value the contribution of the content to whatever the cause may be. Another might be how often the page is shared or referenced by supporters or others looking for information on your topic.

FEEDBACK

"Here are a few ways to measure impact:

- Direct Measurable Impact
- External Measurable Impact
- Measurable Next Steps
- Anecdotal Response
- Increased Engagement
- Raw Views"

MEASURABLE NEXT STEPS

Sometimes the content we create doesn't have a specific ask. One way to measure in the digital space is to lead people deeper into your site. If a page has a high exit or bounce rate, you may want to consider revising or deleting it. If you can clearly see a connection from one piece of content to a next step or another information page, then that may be a worthwhile impact.

ANECDOTAL RESPONSE

Sometimes when we are pushing on a target like a company, politician, or institution, we have to look at movement from them as a goal. If you are trying to move one of these targets, is there a way to infer if it hit the mark? You might know you moved them if, after launching, someone from the target group confirmed a meeting to discuss next steps, or if they released a statement on the issue you are pushing. It could even be your messaging or a rebuttal appearing in their communications.

An internal anecdotal response could be hearing from supporters about how it changes their feeling or connection to the organization, campaign, or issue.

INCREASED ENGAGEMENT

If you have the luxury of a system that captures data well, you can seek correlations between certain pieces or types of content you produce with other actions like donations or volunteering.

If you don't have that luxury, look for patterns where content (and content referenced) connects to, supports, and leads them to further engagement.

RAW VIEWS

At the very least, set a number of page views you might want for the content. If you believe the content is clearly moving the needle on your impact, then decide what number of page views would look like a success. Set a value for the number of views you need to move forward in a meaningful way. Would having 100 or 1,000 views that engage supporters over a month be worth the content being produced? To get to an answer there, you might need to dig into a bit of your own site's historical analytics. Make sure it is about moving your clear campaign goals and how these views get you closer.

Right Content and Layout

Now that you have the right audience and right impact, you just need to connect to the right content. This is where Right Audience + Right Impact + Right Content and Layout = Change.

It really is all about the combination of content and layout. Make sure you've thought through things like supporting imagery and video.

To choose the right content, pick the one main message this piece needs to convey. Back to goals—what is the goal of this piece? How will you deliver it to the audience? Keep thinking about the goals while going through production. More often than not, you can simplify and let good content be good content.

Once you have clearly written down main message, audience and impact, make sure you clearly understand your container. This is why content and layout are twin pillars. Are you drafting petition information that is normally less than 300 words or are you drafting a long-form story? Make sure you understand how you are going to introduce and close the content.

Think through the layout of all content, I really mean it, apply this to all site content. Too often, folks don't apply this thinking to simple pages like donate pages. My experience time and time again is when you apply good content theory to all content, you increase engagement. Does the donate page language match whatever content may have taken the user there? Is it still clear why this action matters? Is it simple enough to skim and take the action? If not, there must be a really compelling reason to lower conversions. Maybe you have a special fund and you need to make very clear to supporters exactly where the money is going. It might be worth dropping your conversion rate by a few percentage points if the long run experience is better.

While I can't offer a silver bullet on how to layout your content, I can offer a few simple tips to help you make decisions. Look at others doing what you want to do. Especially look at well funded larger entities. Do you want to know who spends a lot of time worrying about users reading to the end of an article? Media companies. You want to know who spends a lot of time page conversions and donations? Look at the bigger organizations in your field. Learn, model, and test what works for you.

Blogs

There are so many great things you can do with a thoughtful blog. Many organizations rarely answer the questions: Why do you have to have a blog? Why? What purpose does it serve your organization? Even

BRAINSTORM AND PLAN

"All too often, we hear just write a blog about it. The outcome reads as poorly as middle school *that's what I did last summer* essays.

Put some actual brainstorming and planning in and respect both you and your supporters' time."

if your organization has had a blog and you are thinking about revamping it, then you should what the goal of your blog is. Here are a few ways to approach blogs:

- The Catch-All blog, this is what most organizations use and, while I won't fault you for it because of capacity, the reality is they are rarely engaging.
- Storytelling blog, now this is where organizations connect with people.
- Issue/Department/Function Themed Blog, when done well is an expansion of storytelling to cover broader issues and topics.

Thinking through any of the following approaches and uses could be fine depending on your organization, but you should know what you intend to do with it. Otherwise, consider opting out of it. That's okay too. But remember when done well, blogs are an important piece in an ecosystem of content and engagement.

THE CATCH-ALL BLOG

Most organizations just put up random information and they don't intend to post as stand-alone pages to their blog. It works if that's your only goal. If you are hoping to inspire readership don't expect it to catch one. No one wants to wade through your press releases, stories, organizational funding updates, and programmatic changes in the same stream. Would you read that? I wouldn't. The individual pieces might get life if you share them via email or social media, but you aren't likely to see return readership. That's okay as long as you know this is your goal and expectation.

STORYTELLING BLOG

These are rare. But some organizations do find a way to write a compelling ongoing narrative about the organization. When done well, they will certainly raise organizational engagement and affinity. You will need to have a really functional content production calendar and system for remaining consistent. It takes an investment in time (and possible staff) which is inherently money to organizations.

ISSUE/DEPARTMENT/FUNCTION THEMED BLOG

Most blogs I see look a little more like this. It is a hard model to either break away from or make great. Organizations often do many things and they want to tell the story of them all. You might use tags and categories to try and make the content feel connected.

I have yet to see the connection link into a coherent narrative. Most likely you'll be relying on the one-off pieces of content being driven by other engagement channels. Here you should still be thinking about how you close individual blog posts to get the impact you want. A link to another article or action or donation for instance.

While at RAN, we began a long journey into restructuring our content into ways that allowed people to read a piece of content and see how it fit into broader issues and campaigns. NGO and political campaigns are so often geared to just the linear timeline and workflow that it makes shifting how we produce and manage content difficult. So how do you create content that is a narrative people can drop into and go deeper if they want to? Although campaigns internally function in a linear way, every day there will (or should) be new people making a connection to the issue or organization. How do you get them up to speed and engaged in a meaningful way? Certainly a mishmash of not concretely related content linked via tags is not the way. I truly believe organizations that tackle those questions will unlock greater engagement than they ever have before. Have a long view of goals and campaigns, and structure your blogs in a way that make it easy to connect to information over time. This allows users to drop in and connect to an issue in a fluid way. This will inherently expand your engagement and move the needles greatly toward your goals.

Storytelling

Gathered around the campfire, the radio, the TV, the laptop, and mobile device, humans find themselves most drawn to story. Storytelling is a cross-cultural human experience so why do organizations keep trying to move people with facts and process? More often than not, the individuals in organizations who manage policy and campaigns, feel deeply connected to an issue. They themselves are deeply swayed by facts. It is true, there is a subset of the human population more swayed by facts than story. But the reality is, this subset is smaller than the audience you most likely need to make change.

Great digital work empowers storytelling across platforms, expands audiences, and creates greater impact. It is a thing you can strategically plan for.

The following sections are a few ways to embrace storytelling.

HUMAN SCALE OF A MAJOR ISSUE

All too often, issues feel beyond our impact. Take climate change or gun violence, for example. When stated by name, these issues feel wildly beyond one's ability to change anything. If you stay in the big statistics and facts, it is overwhelming. To move people, hone in on one specific story, (yes, in a single piece of content) and try to keep it to one.

Don't go light touch on several stories crammed into one piece of content. Pick one that illustrates the problem. It is okay to weave in the bigger statistics but you need to express them in a way that the reader can relate on a human level.

For climate change, for example, can you connect people to someone immediately impacted? Don't hang in the space of the entire community. Use the community to get even closer. Find a way to describe what these immediate impacts mean, such as how unstable life is, how it feels, and how those feelings ripple into every aspect of life. Then present the possibility of change in a realistic manner. Link that human-level story to what's next for the person in the story so that the reader can find connection.

READER AS ALLY

You can create a narrative about impact humans, the ones making change on issues, where the reader can clearly draw a line as an ally. Can you show impact from others like the reader? Find a way to make it clear that there is a way to be supportive. Don't leave folks in the gloom of the story, but make it clear there is a way to be supportive with time or funding.

READER AS CHANGE AGENT

The reader as a change agent works best when you can model the behaviors of another. Like the story of about Obama volunteers above. It was a place where the narrative wasn't about Obama or leaders in Washington D.C. but everyday people working for change. Find that story you can tell that allows some to vividly see what it would look like for them to be a change agent.

Tell a story that includes common barriers. Barriers could be time, money, systemic pressure. Find a way to walk the reader through the way in which someone else overcame such barriers. In these stories, don't reach for the super-heroic; that's a hard place for others to see themselves. Go for the common everyday person and leave the super-heroic for the ally stories where someone wants to support the heroine or hero. Find those ordinary traits and emphasize those.

ENGAGE

"There are so many ways to engage your audience with good storytelling.

Stop writing dry essays or soulless report backs. Decide who your audience is and engage them."

HEROES AND VILLAINS

A tried and true storytelling device is creating two clear sides and one clear villain. In this story format, you make clear the heroic traits of the individual, team, or organization you want readers to align with. You then cast the opposition as a villain where reviled traits are clear.

I have to be honest—Heroes and Villains isn't my favorite storytelling approach. Not because it doesn't work, but because I think so much of what is a mess in the current state of American politics is an oversimplified use of this storytelling device. There is an inherent polarization that happens with this kind of story.

If you want to draw a distinct line, this is a very powerful device, hence its rapid use in the media narrative. You should also know that when used, it is hard to walk back from painting someone as a villain. But if long-run relationships aren't important, think about how you can pull on traits of hero and villain. Tug them and make it clear your reader can be part of the heroic team. This could be used either in how they are an ally to the heroes or how they themselves are an agent of the rebel alliance.

Summary

Take time and be intentional about site content and the layout you choose so you can achieve the impact you want. Blogs can serve many functions and you can strategically think about the ways a blog can highlight your organization, your work, your theory of change, and meet your goals. It is up to you to be strategic about your approach. You can tie it all together with storytelling and narrative. Being thorough in thinking about the Right Audience, Right Impact, Right Content and Layout will mean finding a path through storytelling. That path will help you achieve your goals.

Stories and Studies

Presented by Katrina Mendoza, Michael Stein,
Emily Katz and Caitlin Mitchell.

Stories Bend Us and Bind Us

KATRINA MENDOZA // CEO, *Ditch The Box Studios* //
k.alexandramendoza@gmail.com

Since the dawn of time, humans have been gathering to share stories. As an embedded survival mechanism, stories were used to pass on valuable knowledge of resources, as well as to warn and protect others from danger. Though stories are now more complex, colorful and creative, they still hold the same power to make a memorable impact.

I'm a filmmaker, storyteller, and activist. My entire life has been an exploration of communication and I've learned some powerful lessons through my Master's program, working in the entertainment, tech and nonprofit industries, and then building a video production business focused on community impact. I carry these lessons with me every day because communication happens with every interaction through energetic exchange including body language, words, sounds and tones, gestures, emotional mood and stories. Remember that communication is complex, and you'll understand why a video is more powerful than a blog post. Not just because its interactivity level is the closest you can get to face-to-face (the most powerful form of communication), but you can also share stories with video in new and interesting ways when you integrate color, music, titles and contrasting elements.

To tell a powerful story, keep it simple and close to your heart. Pull from your own emotional experiences and clarify the purpose of the story you tell by knowing how you want folks to feel when the story is done. The emotional impact you make is where the power of story shines. Maya Angelou really said it best, "I have learned that people will forget what you said, people will forget what you did, but people will never forget how you make them feel."

Know that every element of your story contributes to the overall feeling of the piece. Focus on the feeling, and all the other elements will fall into place.

Listening to Data: Turning Analytics Into Engagement

MICHAEL STEIN // Principal, *Oakwood Digital* // @mstein63
EMILY KATZ // Director, *Northern California Grantmakers* // www.ncg.org

It's an open secret in many professions and sectors: visitors to our websites ignore our lovingly curated stories, and head straight to our job listings. This case study is about Northern California Grantmakers, which brings together foundations, nonprofit organizations, government, and business to tackle the region's most pressing social issues. NCG has over 200 organizations as members who collectively bring deep expertise across a wide range of issues including health, education, arts, immigration, workforce, environment and much more.

This project involved doing a deep dive into NCG's digital engagement data. We reviewed website, email and social data, trying to decrypt the traffic flows. We were fascinated by the fact that web traffic to the site's public job board eclipsed all the other web pages combined. Without an intentional strategy, NCG's website was attracting talent for the philanthropy sector. Visitors—who are not NCG members—loved our website for professional opportunities in philanthropy.

From this core observation emerged a conversation about engagement with our non-member website visitors. What would happen if NCG were to welcome these visitors and connect them with the people making things happen and the latest thinking on how to make the change we're all seeking?

Thus NCG's e-magazine, Together For Good, was born—a bi-weekly e-newsletter with a companion "online magazine" on the NCG website that highlights stories of people making philanthropy happen in the Northern California region as well as insights on how to do our jobs better, news from their members, and the latest research.

The Jobs Board pages got a user experience redesign, making sign-ups easy, and infusing the e-magazine's identity throughout NCG's communications channels, and thereby creating an easy way for non-members to stay up-to-date with the Northern California philanthropy community.

A year into this engagement shift, we've continued to listen to the data to deepen the organization's learning process around engagement and storytelling:

- Our email list has grown at a steady five percent per month, as new subscribers come on board, driven principally by the continued strong traffic to the NCG website "Job Board."

- We've sustained strong email open and click-through rates, demonstrating continued interest in this model of people and career-centered content.
- Posts about people—getting hired, changing jobs, retiring, being honored, sharing a view—outperform everything else.
- Finally, we get great feedback from people in our community. It allowed us to engage with our members and a broader audience in a new way—bringing together great people who are doing great work through shared narratives.

The *Together for Good* analytics project highlights the importance of using analytics to hear and respond to what stakeholders are telling us. The goal of connecting and learning about each other has resonated with many people in the Northern California philanthropy community, and demonstrated the true power of storytelling.

Best Practice: The Case for Emotion

CAITLIN MITCHELL // Chief Mobilization Officer, *Democratic National Committee* // @k8thegr8est

I don't mean to go all squishy on you, but I'd like to share a few words on feelings. Emotions, to be exact.

As a digital practitioner with a decade of experience writing and managing writers, I can tell you that **no digital trick, tactic, or testing is as important as the emotion at the heart of every message you send.** And this is coming from someone who loves tricks, tactics, and testing. Sure, we can write informative content that fully explains a political issue, exactly where it is in the legislative process, how many votes we need for it to pass or fail, and pair it with a nice optimized ask. As communicators, it's natural to want to tell the whole story. But this content often doesn't move supporters to take action, and I can tell you why: it lacks emotion.

And donating, volunteering, and speaking out are all emotionally-based decisions.

So here's a trick I've used with teams from OFA to EMILY's List to the DNC. Before an email draft or social post is ever written, choose the emotion you're trying to convey, put it at the top of your draft, and write from there. It may sound hokey, but it works.

Sometimes identifying that emotion is easy, take for example, Congress passing a tax bill that's essentially a giant giveaway to wealthy Americans and corporations that screws over everyone else. The emotion here is outrage, in that in case, it's important for you to match the outrage that a supporter is probably already feeling. Go too far, and you'll turn a supporter off. They might be angry, but not that angry. Don't go far enough, and you're not going to move them to action. They'll still feel the way they do, but your call to action, whatever it may be, is not going to help them resolve it.

Sometimes, finding the emotion is harder—especially around issues that haven't gotten a lot of public attention or interest, or that you may not initially know much about. In that case, your job is to find the driving emotion that will bring a supporter to care, and move them to get there. There's a catch, though: The emotion has to be authentic. Fake outrage, empathy, or frustration is commonplace in digital content—and easily spotted. Take the time to learn about an issue and consider the angles until you find what resonates with you—that's what you should write about, even if it's not commonly discussed or at the top of the talking points.

Finally, sometimes you may need to write about something that isn't going to happen for days or weeks later, or to write quickly on a topic when the emotion you're going for couldn't be further from your mind. A personal example: write a heartfelt, inspiring email from Barack Obama that will be the first thing supporters see the morning of Election Day to remind them to go vote, but write it in the office, at midnight, a week before Election Day. **In situations like this, I recommend music—or if it works better for you, a movie clip.** Find the emotion you want to convey, then think of the closest song or movie scene that portrays it. Listen to it or watch it, as many times as you need, until you feel it. Then write.

Yes, this is like the Method Acting of writing, but if you don't believe what you're writing, why should anyone else? You may end up with Bruce Springsteen's "Born to Run" stuck in your head for weeks like I did after writing that email from Barack Obama, but you'll also end up with a lot better content than simply telling people it's time to go vote.

SMS (SHORTCODE)

This chapter is presented by Lloyd Cotler.
Solutions Architect // *Hustle* // @lloydcotler

Email and social media may have a wide reach, but broadcast SMS is the best way to build relationships with a large community of supporters.

How to use this chapter

Non-Digital Leadership or Management: This chapter is important to help you think about the power and likely untapped potential SMS holds for your organization.

Digital/Tech staffers: Practical knowledge to help you think about how SMS links into many elements of digital and tech strategy.

New Staff/Activists: Worth getting an understanding of, but can be harder to scale for small groups because of costs.

KEY TAKEAWAYS AND ELEMENTS:
- Strategic insight for how to use SMS to drive engagement and fundraise
- Clarity on broadcast SMS and peer-to-peer text messaging
- Strategic insights in the value of SMS and possible ways to have a campaign pay for itself

Before getting into strategies and tactics to build and successfully run a broadcast SMS program, we have to define what it is first, since it's still unfamiliar terrain for many digital organizers.

Broadcast SMS programs run on shortcodes (five or six digit phone numbers); they have strict opt-in requirements; they are generally automated, prompting users to respond in specific ways to advance conversations; and they are regulated by the CTIA (Cellular Telephone Industry Association) and the FCC (Federal Communications Commission) in accordance with the Telephone Consumer Protection Act of 1991 (TCPA.) These programs can also include but are distinct from text-to-give, which allows users to make donations through carrier billing.

SMS programs can be on dedicated codes, in which an organization or campaign is the only one with a specific shortcode, or a shared short code, in which many groups use the same code to keep costs down. If you are serious about running a top-notch SMS program, you should absolutely invest in a dedicated code. It will open up all opt-in keywords for you, make it easier for you to interact with users who make errors in automated flows, and give you an easier time branding. Dedicated codes can also be random digits or a vanity code, which you choose. Generally speaking vanity codes are an unnecessary expense, as no one uses T9 texting anymore.

Your vendor will typically procure your shortcode, or put you on a shared short code with other customers. You can procure one yourself as well, if you build your program on Twilio directly. This is an advanced setup—most people use a vendor's platform. Your vendor should also offer compliance guidance.

Planning Your Program and Building Your List

The first thing you need to think about before starting a broadcast SMS program is "how am I going to grow this list?" Remember, every person on your list needs to opt-in, so you can't simply add your database of cell phone numbers and start texting.

At first blush that can seem daunting—after all, it's taken you years to build your email list and social media audiences. But remember, literally everyone else who has built an SMS program also started from scratch. Your email list started at zero. Like anything else, you just need to give people a reason to sign up your texts.

It should go without saying for any digital marketer, but you need to give people a reason to get your texts, so you should brainstorm what you want your program to look like before launch. Then you can accurately advertise, and see lower churn if you give people what they expect. Groups and campaigns that simply advertise "join our SMS list" or "sign up for text alerts" fall very short in terms of acquisition compared to those that ask you to join for exclusive content, urgent actions, or other compelling reasons.

So what do you want to use your list for? Your number one answer here should be fundraising. By virtue of having strict opt-in requirements, your SMS list will contain many of your most active and highest performing supporters. Your priority should be maximizing their donations to help raise money to offset the cost of the program. Of course, telling people to sign up for texts so you can ask them for money isn't a very compelling pitch—so you need think about what else you're doing and pitch that.

You might offer exclusive content to SMS subscribers and have them be the first to find out important updates or offer them opportunities to get their questions answered in a one-on-one setting. You can give behind the scenes looks at events or campaigns, tell stories interactively, or crowdsource photos and stories. Ideally, you should be doing it all.

Now that you've got an idea of what you want to do, how do you actually start? Do you need a huge event to launch your list, and when is that going to happen? Don't wait. Just start building so that you're already ready to activate your list when something happens.

The single most important thing you can do to grow your SMS list, is to add mobile phone and SMS opt-in fields to your web forms. Adding these fields do not lower your conversion rates by any significant degree, and the increased value of SMS subscribers more than outweighs any lost conversions.

Once you've done that, start getting creative. Emails to your list framing the SMS list as a next-level action are a great start, as are some social media share graphics. Different keywords for your different channels let you source where your opt-ins are coming from, and subsequently target users for interactions based on their initial channel. For example, you might want to ask all your subscribers who opted-in after a tweet to use a particular hashtag for an event. Ask your subscribers to tell their friends to join with a dedicated "tell-a-friend" ask at the end of an action.

Look to the field, where an SMS opt-in ask is going to be more effective than asking people to visit your website from a stage or house party. Add your keywords to signs, placards, banners, stickers and anywhere else you have real estate.

SMS acquisition is also a powerful way to convert channels you might spend a lot of time working on content for (YouTube, Instagram, Snapchat) but that don't have ways of converting people into action takers. By directing your social audiences to your SMS list, you can sign them up for much more valuable interactions later.

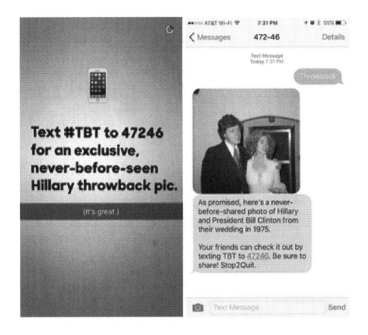

Think about groups and potential constituencies you're not reaching, and how SMS might change that. Campuses are huge pools of potential mobile subscribers you're missing from your email list. Give celebrity endorsers their own keywords to share in other channels so you can report big their exact influence on your program.

The possibilities for list growth are endless—and as you'll see below, running a good list will net you more subscribers through positive word of mouth and social sharing.

DEVELOPING YOUR VOICE

The other big decision you have to make when you start your program is who is going to be the voice of your list. You might send emails to supporters from many different senders, but text messages should come from a single voice. The single phone number, the history of messages, the iPhone functionality of guessing the sender, and the importance of building a relationship via SMS all support a single voice. For reasons that will become apparent later, it is strongly suggested that this is a real person and not a fictional personality you create for staff members to assume.

WHAT CONTENT WORKS

SMS is a really different beast than email or social media, and your content strategy needs to reflect that. Unlike email, your supporters will probably see every (or at the very least, a vast majority) of your messages so you can't send nearly the same volume. Unlike social media, your texts will appear chronologically instead of sorted by an algorithm. This means you have an ongoing, consistent relationship with supporters and can actually converse with them. SMS can also feel like a safe place for supporters—they can interact with you and not face trolls or harassment online, so you can be a little more personal.

SMS is going to be the best tool in your toolbox for rapid response. Because your list is going to be made up in part of your strongest supporters, use SMS to arm them with whatever they need for your rapid response strategy. Whether it's information they need, information they should share, a hit on an opponent, or something they need to raise money for—when you send out an important update your list is going to respond.

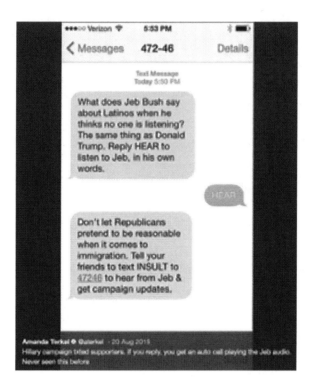

Speaking of raising money, your SMS list is going to be a major boost to your fund-raising. The Hillary for America SMS list made over 9x the cost of the program in small dollar donations. As paying for things with your cell phone becomes more ubiquitous, the more your supporters will be familiar with making donations from their phones.

There was almost no type of donation ask via SMS that didn't perform well. Whether the ask came from Jess from HFA or from Hillary herself, whether the ask was robotic and automated or warm and personal, whether it was urgent or not—your list sees every message you send, and they care enough about your cause or candidate to react.

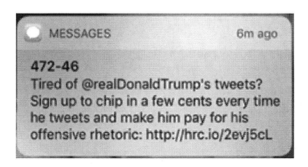

Obviously, you should make your SMS donations as frictionless as possible—pass profile parameters through a URL to fill out form fields where you can, or if you're able to integrate directly with your donation processor to enable quick SMS donations. At HFA, a tool was built specifically for this purpose, but a similar set up is available through some vendors and ActBlue Express Lane.

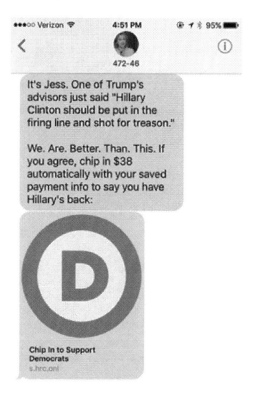

Overall, 50% of the HFA SMS list donated at least once and 40% saved their credit card info for quick donations.

Furthermore, the intimate nature of SMS means you can convert non-donors with some simple touches. When non-donors received a $1 ask and replied "what does $1 possibly do?" or similar, a simple canned response telling supporters that their donation helped pay for the platform to send the text messages converted over 1/3 of people into $5 donations—a 500% upsell from a single reply. Often just confirming for users that you're a real person and not a robot means significant buy-in from them.

The biggest problem organizations often face doing SMS fundraising, is a reticence to ask. It can sometimes feel off-putting to interrupt people and ask them for money. It's true—you'll get some opt-outs! But you get opt-outs from fundraising emails too, and you still send those. The opt-out rates will also be lower than you might expect—the fact that supporters see every message you send means they have a better view of the whole picture, and are more willing to forgive a bad or annoying message here and there.

Next up, your SMS list is going to be great at mobilizing your supporters to take offline action. You're communicating with people on their mobile phone—that means they can move. Get them to events and actions, or show them a picture message of what they're missing. You can also mobilize people quickly, like when you get a text from a friend about something happening right now.

Here is an example of where your broadcast and peer-to-peer programs can interact—ask supporters to reply that they're interested in taking action, and then message them from a peer-to-peer platform to introduce them to a local organizer and recruit them with a more personal touch.

And if you're staging an event quickly, send a picture message of where you're located to urge locals to join you.

Another somewhat counterintuitive strength of broadcast SMS is storytelling. Despite the limited character count, you can set up complicated and lengthy call-and-response message flows, breaking up stories and explainers into digestible bites. You can include gifs and images to liven up your flow, and be out quicker and with fewer resources than if you needed to make a video.

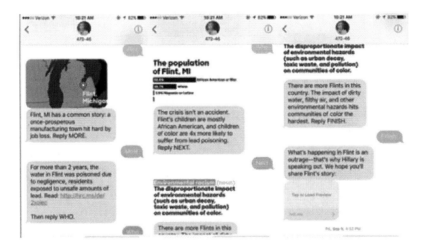

Open your SMS list up to questions from your supporters about topics they care about, or things they might be confused about. Hillary for America answered hundreds of thousands of questions about voting during both the primary and general elections—things like, "can I bring my child to the caucus?" or "will there be a sign language translator?" meant running an inclusive campaign, maximizing turnout, and giving a positive touch to some of our most dedicated supporters.

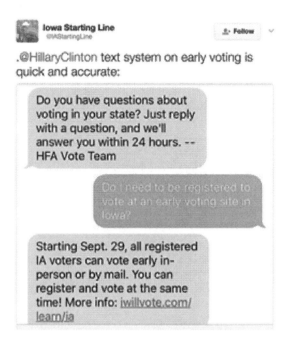

Others have used the Q&A style to do office hours with supporters, opening themselves up to questions about strategy, legislation, policy and more. Promote your office hours on social media to your audiences there, giving them a chance to talk with you, while also protecting them from trolls and online harassment.

If you have a Spanish-speaking audience, SMS is another avenue you should explore—especially if you don't have the staff time to devote to maintaining a Spanish language site and social accounts. Funnel your Spanish-speaking audience to your SMS list (which will be easier—Spanish-only speakers are more likely to text and less likely to have consistent internet access than many other groups) and keep them updated and engaged with considerably fewer resources.

POLITICS

Hillary Clinton campaign steps up to protect Latino voters with new hotline in Spanish

Jorge Rivas
10/06/16 11:02am · Filed to: AMERICAS ⌄

SPL|NTER

Finally, SMS is a great medium to just have fun in. You're dealing with mostly your best supporters and your youngest. You can lean into the strengths of texting like sending reaction gifs, asking people to take selfies during actions, or play trivia games while waiting for events to start. You want your subscribers to enjoy getting texts from you—experiment a little bit with what makes them happy.

MAKE YOUR SMS LIST THE PLACE WHERE PEOPLE LOOK FOR BIG MOMENTS

If you have a big moment or campaign event, center your hype around your SMS list. Hillary for America told people to subscribe for texts to be among the first to learn who the vice presidential candidate would be, and promoted the opt-in code and short code at every opportunity. Anticipation built and people were talking not only about the candidate, but the SMS list as well. The growth was exponential and because people had signed up for weeks preceding the announcement, they got to know "Jess" and didn't opt-out at any significant rate following the announcement text they had initially signed up for.

DON'T FORGET TO INTERACT WITH YOUR SUBSCRIBERS

Just because it's called *broadcast* SMS doesn't mean it has to be one-way communication. Most platforms have a one-on-one response feature, and you should use it. Create canned responses for commonly asked questions ('are you a real person?') and take the time to respond thoughtfully to people who ask serious questions or express real concerns. Unless you're a presidential campaign you probably don't need to spend more than an hour a day replying to supporters.

You can also use your SMS list to gather content for your other lists. Ask supporters to send in selfies from campaigns and create Facebook albums full of their photos. Add a template to your SnapChat or Instagram stories and encourage audiences to screenshot it, add their own spin, and send it back to you to post. Gather responses to text asks and make a blog post of them, reporting back to your list and showing people what they're missing out on by not subscribing.

Finally, don't limit your interactions to SMS. You are a real person who exists—when you see people tweeting about your texts, tweet back at them! If you see them questioning whether you're a robot, show them you're not.

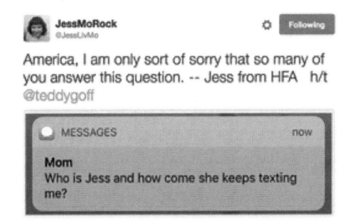

JessMoRock
@JessLivMo

Following

America, I am only sort of sorry that so many of you answer this question. -- Jess from HFA   h/t @teddygoff

> MESSAGES   now
>
> **Mom**
> Who is Jess and how come she keeps texting me?

INTERACTING WITH YOUR PEER-TO-PEER PROGRAM

I mentioned earlier one way of using your different SMS platforms in tandem—recruiting volunteers by broadcast SMS and then following up with them by peer-to-peer. But you can also use your peer-to-peer program to recruit for your broadcast list. Set up a dedicated keyword and message flow for these people to offer them something unique for joining, and make clear the differences between the two programs.

You should also remember that most peer-to-peer platforms will permanently opt subscribers out if they don't wish to be contacted again, while broadcast SMS lets users re-subscribe if they like. If your peer-to-peer contacts express some skepticism about getting texts, offer them the chance to get your shortcode messages instead so they can opt-in and out as they please.

You can also think of these two platforms as entirely distinct and discrete—peer-to-peer texting often lives with the field team, while broadcast SMS lives in digital, and that structure works for many organizations and campaigns. You don't have to force them to interact if it doesn't work for you, but it's important to note for yourself and others that it isn't either/or with SMS strategies.

TESTING

Testing around your SMS list can be tricky, since you are often working with smaller universes than when you test email, social, or ads.

Things you should test are:

- **Frequency.** Text messages cost money. If you can do more by sender fewer texts, that's great. If you can send a lot of messages and keep strong fundraising numbers, that's great too. But make sure to test frequency of messages to find the right balance between sending too many texts and not sending enough.
- **Tell-a-friends.** If your vendor's platform has a tell-a-friend tool where your subscriber enters their friends' phone numbers to invite them, test that against giving your supporters a dedicated tell-a-friend keyword to share on social media. Subscribers who join via tell-a-friend are consistently some of the best performers, so maximizing their join rate is key.
- **Personalization.** Does including a first name or other information increase response rates or donations? If not, don't bother with it. Merging in profile fields often slow send times and can contain mistakes, so if it doesn't help don't bother.
- **Everything around fundraising.** Different types of donation pages (2-step vs. 3-step, for instance); different payment types (Apple Pay, PayPal, ActBlue); different voices (your regular sender vs. an automated-looking message); and anything else you're able to.
- **SMS vs. email acquisition.** If you're paying for ads, test the value of email vs. SMS signups to get the most out of your ad money.
- **Cannibalization.** Are your SMS donors just moving their donations from email to SMS? That's a net loss for you, since texts cost more than emails do. Or are you tapping a new vein, getting money you otherwise wouldn't?

Things you should not bother testing are:
- **Time of day.** A lot of people get hung up on what is the best time to send messages. The truth is that people read texts very quickly no matter what time of the day you send them (unless they're asleep), and your message should be compelling and urgent enough to get them to act regardless of what time it is.
- **MMS vs. SMS.** Unless it's really important that you're sending a picture message, don't bother. Send times are slower, MMS messages cost more, and they haven't been shown to have any significant impact on conversions. In fact, some users might not even see them if they don't have a phone or plan that supports picture messaging.
- **Slightly varied wording, link placement, and other small changes** that may be useful for email testing but is unlikely going to have an impact on your SMS program.

BEST PRACTICES

Best practices around your SMS list are always evolving, especially as Apple makes updates. During the 2016 campaign, we had to make adjustments as iPhones started recognizing "Maybe: Jess" as the sender, or removing the visible link and replacing it with a page preview.

You want to text people like they are your friends—don't use stilted language, or recycle tweets as texts. You're not talking at subscribers like you are on Twitter—you're talking with them.

Don't always ask people for things. You're building a relationship with people, it doesn't have to be purely transactional. Remember, since you're a real person, you can do real person things like wish your subscribers happy holidays or just say thanks.

Respond to people. Try to get back to people within 24 hours, and monitor your inbox after a broadcast, especially for events and other offline activities. You want to be able to monitor and resolve anything that could block your supporters from taking action. If you can't commit to responding in 24 hours, give your supporters an idea of when they'll hear back from you.

WHERE BROADCAST SMS COMES UP SHORT

Broadcast SMS is awesome at a lot of things, but like everything else, it has its shortcomings and deltas.

Voter registration and Election Day GOTV work are often huge time-sucks because the differences between every state mean nearly 60 different flows each time you need to do a round of outreach, in some cases for very small pools of voters. If people are subscribed to your SMS list, the chances that they're already registered to vote are very high—don't spend a lot of time on trying to register them again.

For GOTV, focus on converting your list into early voters if possible rather than turning them out on Election Day, freeing them up to volunteer to help with your GOTV efforts.

You also might be tempted to send a lot of picture messages or graphics, especially if you're doing rapid response and have content you created for social media. Fight that urge. Sending MMS at a large scale slows down your send speeds, making your rapid response significantly less rapid. No test has shown that MMS messages perform better than regular SMS messages, and they increase your costs. MMS should be reserved for small sends or very important updates—or you should be asking your supporters to send photos to you instead.

Strong SMS campaigns aren't limited to big campaigns and organizations. Anyone can build strong, active programs to raise money, turn out supporters, and connect constituents to their representatives regardless of their constituencies, location, or size.

Stories and Studies

Presented by Hillary Lehr, Amy Leaman, and Salim Zymet.

Fearless Early Adoption Gets Results

HILLARY LEHR // VP of Client Success, *Hustle* // @HillaryLehr

When I joined the Hustle team in the beginning of 2016, the concept of 'peer-to-peer text' was brand spankin' new. How would we prove out this concept, and once we did, how would we create best practices for this entirely brand new toolset? While broadcast SMS messaging had been around for several years, we were still in the early product development stages to create a new type of tool that would allow organizers to rapidly send hundreds of personalized, individual texts from a real, local phone number. Why has it taken off? Results. When an organizer reaches out personally over text, people reply and they show up.

Creative Conversions Using One-on-One SMS Outreach

AMY LEAMAN // Co-founder and Creative Director, *C Street* // @cstreet_ca

Our digital organizing agency had the privilege to work with Jagmeet Singh, the first person of color to be elected as leader of a major party in Canada: the progressive New Democratic Party. In order to win the leadership, his team embraced the opportunity to bring in thousands of new members to the party from racialized communities across the country. All new members had to sign up through the party website, and then membership lists were sent to the candidates. This meant there was no way to know the conversion rate of outreach to membership.

We knew we needed people to complete an interim step without discouraging sign up, so we created a landing page on Jagmeet's website that captured only name and email before redirecting them to the party membership page. Then, his team cross-referenced the membership list against their sign-ups, and used Hustle to outreach one-to-one via SMS to the people who dropped off. They signed up over 47,000 new party members, tripling the party membership, and winning the leadership on the first ballot in a four-person race. The key was creating a low barrier to entry and then using one-to-one outreach to ask people to do that next, harder thing.

Be Authentic and Results Will Follow

HILLARY LEHR // VP of Client Success, *Hustle* // @HillaryLehr

Following Hustle's early success with the Bernie Sanders and Hillary Clinton campaigns in the 2016 primaries, we began to explore long-term grassroots organizing possibilities with large organizations like FWD.us, Everytown for Gun Safety, and Planned Parenthood. The excitement and patience of our early users were remarkable, and their feedback was instrumental in every next step of development. We oriented Hustle's product around really strong user feedback and noticed patterns of how early Hustlers used the tool. For example, Lauren Banker was an organizer in New Hampshire who decided to use Hustle's Event Invitation tool to ask local supporters to phone a local decision-maker regarding funding for a local health center. She used the reply fields to text the representative's office phone number and followed up again with supporters to confirm if they made the call. By doing so, Lauren was able to confirm that over 30 supporters made calls and the vote was victorious—funding was restored! For local decision-makers, 30 phone calls is a LOT, and we found that text helped bridge between online and offline engagement in a way that built relationships and drove action. Based on this experience, our product team ended up building a "Legislative Contact" goal type that helped organizers make call-in action asks and track the number of calls placed. All thanks to Lauren's creative use of Hustle!

Our team is filled with trainers from a progressive organizing background, we knew that we wanted to provide as much training, support, and best practice documentation as we could for our partners. I can't say enough how important it is for any technology company to hire and support diverse teams that understand the space from the get-go. It is a responsibility we have and keep to this day, and this is most efficient for product feedback, use cases, and training material creation, as well as roadmap development.

To help affiliated organizations adopt Hustle to learn how people were using the tool, and to begin to really hone in on what was working, we set up monthly working group calls where affiliates could share 'Home Runs' and ask one another for advice. This created natural leadership and comfort with new tools across the organization, and it helped our client success team understand where people got stuck or would benefit from new features. These calls also helped us create case studies to build enthusiasm, demonstrate truly phenomenal increases in engagement and turnout, and early best practices. When a team member has the opportunity to own a result and be proud of progress then they will keep using the tool. It makes their life easier and helps them be great at what they do. Winning!

The Number 1 factor in peer-to-peer texting success lies in one thing: <u>authenticity.</u>

The best practices associated with this involve keeping text messages feeling like texts: short, sweet, and casual! This is *not* email folks, no need with formalities over here. To get in the habit of creating peer-to-peer text messages that feel like texts, I highly recommend pulling out your phone and typing up a message to a contact in your phonebook with your ask. Use that as your script. Feel free to use emojis and abbreviations. Introduce yourself and most importantly: make sure your teams reply quickly. We recommend within 30 minutes, tops.

As our team grew, we got the additional capacity to crunch the data to look at trends. In some initial analysis, we have found that emojis can increase reply rates by 3.5%! We've also seen that of all MMS types, GIFs outperform still JPEGs in keeping reply rates up and maintaining regular opt-out rates. But all of this depends on context. Your organization, mission, and ask will all affect the type of message that makes the most sense for your supporters. But keep it short, we have found universally, that this keeps your reply rate higher.

At the end of the day, peer-to-peer text is a new method to do old school, tried-and-true organizing: building relationships. Keeping your messaging authentic to yourself as an organizer on behalf of an organization will not only protect the longevity of SMS as a high-impact channel for your communications, it will also add the intimacy and affinity that is at the core of all successful movements: **relationships built around shared values.**

Digital Ads: How Hillary's .25% Iowa Caucus Win May Have Come Down to Digital Ads and SMS

**SALIM ZYMET // Engagement Director, *Crowdpac*
// http://linkedin.com/in/salimzymet**

It was midnight, and we still didn't know who would be winning the Iowa caucus in 2016.
Would Hillary immediately become the front-runner to win the Democratic Nomination?
Would a woman be able to earn her party's nomination for president for the first time in history?

Were all of those 90 hour work weeks worth it?

Thankfully, the answer to all of those questions became a resounding YES when it was announced we had won the caucus by 701 to 697 delegates, or .25%.

But what led to that narrow victory? Which of our tactics effectively moved Iowans to take their entire evening (often upwards of four hours) to meet and talk with their neighbors at a caucus?

While we'll never be able to map out each caucus-goer to that specific moment in time that moved them to caucus, we can make some educated guesses.

First, despite the praises I'm about to sing about our digital program in Iowa, it's no doubt that our victory was 100% owed to the organizers who worked tirelessly across the state, met with caucus-goers, and built our campaign from the ground up in living rooms, meeting halls, and our offices.

Second, with such a small margin, any one tactic could be labeled as "the defining" tactic. We didn't run a campaign like that in Iowa. We were integrated, holistic, and we broke down silos at every turn. Every act fed into another act of organizing and mobilization efforts.

But it's clear that SMS (text) messaging played a key role in informing, mobilizing, and attracting supporters to the campaign.

This piece will take a quick look at a few ways we grew and engaged that list.

Don't Sleep on Offline Recruitment

Every touchpoint you have with a supporter reinforces your value proposition and strengthens your organization. So while you may have a Facebook like or email subscriber who attended a rally or in-person event, you also want them to join your SMS list.

One of the best ways to grow your SMS list is to ask folks to join it in-person. You've seen this before: someone at an event says, "Hey everyone, really quick, pull out your phones. I'll pull mine out my too. I can see you all. I'll wait till there are more phones in the air. OK, awesome. Now, open up your text messaging app and text IOWA to 47246. That's IOWA to 47246. You'll get updates on events near you and we promise we won't text you too often."

The more authentic the messenger (Hillary Clinton!), the better this ask will go, but you'd be surprised how many thousands of people signed up for texts from our rallies.

Use Social Media and Email, Too

You've seen this before, too: instead of posting a link to your landing page, you can post a tweet including the text opt-in. On mediums like Twitter, that's a more native experience than opening a web browser and typing in a bunch of info, and a text subscriber is more valuable than an email subscriber.

Signing up to get "texts from Hillary" was a sexy ask, and we drove a lot of traffic to pages like it.

We also tied SMS opt-in to key events and contests. Want to be entered for a chance to meet Lena Dunham in Iowa? Sign up for text messages.

Want to get a free yard sign? Sign up for text messages. (This one really worked).

Get Creative

Of course, SMS also gives you a ton of flexibility with bot-esque reply flows, short-code text-ins, and media you can send.

In Iowa, we were running an organizer-focused campaign, so we took it to the next level with organizer-specific text opt-ins.

That meant Susan Johnson would have her own unique keyword (something like SusanJ) which she could give to her volunteers and promote online.

This allowed us to easily track how many SMS subscribers came from Susan, and create friendly competition amongst the Iowa caucus team.

How We Used SMS to Mobilize Folks

Once you've got folks on your list, you should ask them to take your most important actions, but try not to text them more than once a week to limit inbox fatigue.

We used our SMS list to build rallies, recruit volunteer shifts, and share breaking news. Timed around key moments (like getting endorsed by the Des Moines register), our engagement via text was through-the-roof and easily outperformed email.

DIGITAL ADS

This section only applies if you have the budget for digital ads, but it may also be the section that helps you make the better case for digital ads.

Let's start with the case for digital ads and how they can impact your goals. Specifically, the power digital ads have to connect to new audiences, reconnect with existing audiences and deepen further connections. Then we'll break down ways to think about ad use when it comes to conversions, impressions, and views. Each outcome is a different goal—the most common outcomes or goals are conversions, impressions, and views. You should frame your strategic plan for digital ads around these goals. We'll pull that together with tips on planning digital ads to make the impact you want.

How to use this chapter

Non-Digital Leadership or Management: Digital advertising is powerful. Getting to know digital ads puts the power in your hands. Digital advertising can create better engagement dollar for dollar against any other format of advertising when done well. It's important to know the fundamentals.

Digital/Tech Staffers: Good digital advertising can involve every facet of digital and tech. You need good copy, design, videos, analytics, a foundation of math, and often good web development to really excel. Knowing the fundamentals can help set you and your organization up for success.

New Staff/Activists: Digital advertising is best when done at scale. It can have small positive impacts but tread lightly to avoid burning the small resources your organization might have.

KEY TAKEAWAYS AND ELEMENTS:
- Understanding the case for digital ads
- Strategic thoughts on reaching new audiences, reconnecting with lapsed audiences, and deepening connection with current audiences
- Clear digital ad planning and budgeting tips

The Case for Digital Ads

Digital ads can help you reach the right audience at the right time. The buzz around digital ads is well deserved, even if somewhat misunderstood. Digital ads aren't a replacement for other good strategies but should be viewed as good argumentation to your other plans. Let's break down how you use digital ads to connect with new audiences, to reconnect or deepen connections, and to influence the influencers.

Reaching New Audiences

Used well, digital ads can allow you to connect to new audiences with precision and focus. First, you need to know who the audience is that you want to reach. If you can identify your target audience, it will be easier to gauge if your ads are performing well. Let's give a concrete example.

Say a number of ads vendors want to focus on a surface level deliverable like CPA (cost per acquisition) of a new email address to your list. If someone says industry standard is $1.50 to $2.00, that sounds like a reasonable metric. And using a number like CPA as a top line metric—the main metric by which you measure success—often makes sense, but how do you know if these emails will be valuable to you?

The questions you need to be able to answer are: what is it you hope cohorts of emails will do

EXECUTE

"Good digital ad execution is a mix of web development, design, analytics, copywriting, and project management. If that sounds overwhelming, consider getting support if you want to do it well."

immediately or over time? Is your goal to build a list of potential donors? Potential online action takers? Something else? Knowing a goal of what you want the new audience to do will let you know if you are on track. If a long-term donation is important to you, then you should be tracking immediate donation (some call it immediate upsell) or long-term donation history of sent emails. An immediate donation from a cohort of ads running is a good indicator if that group is likely to donate in the long run.

Similarly, if you have a particular call to action that is very specific to an issue, you are more likely to get repeat action from those emails. But you might not get a broader organizational connection unless you find ways to connect them through other content using a solid Matrix of Engagement theory.

New audiences can also be people connected with your content including videos, blog posts, and social media graphics. If you are in an awareness-raising phase, ask yourself who you need to reach. Without knowing who it is you need to reach, it is too easy to mismanage a budget for such ads. The power of digital ads allows you to do amazing targeting based on a full range of demographics and interests to see if the ads make the connection you want.

Like no medium before, digital ads let you see results in real time, test, test, and refine your message. Used well, you can test the message and refine based on the actual engagement you get. I do think there are still many reasons to create print mediums (like bumper stickers and signs) and traditional media (like billboards, TV, and radio) because they still have an impact on certain niche audiences. Digital ads empower you to see results with hard statistics and connections, both immediately and with better tracking over time.

Reconnecting

Digital Ads don't just let you connect to new audiences, they also allow you to connect with audiences you have already met. As you probably experience yourself, there are causes you care about, but you miss their content in your Facebook timeline or don't open every email they send. Platforms like Facebook allow you to serve ads back to people who already like you or have stopped responding to emails.

Think about what content might get someone back and feel connected to your cause, and which audience you want to reach with the content. Do you have a cohort of long-time email subscribers that you have some data on about their interests? Is there active content in the form of a sign-up or petition that might get them reactivated? Someone you already have a connection to is likely to be very low hanging fruit.

DEEPENING CONNECTION

The more you can build an affinity between your issue or campaign to a person, the more long-term engagement that is likely to occur. There are so many ways to think about the audience but here are a few to get your ideas flowing.

Your audience is already active, and you want to take it to the next level. Is there a particular cohort of people you have that are active and you want to make another ask of them? Maybe you are worried too many asks may cause them to unsubscribe from your email list. We've all been there—the last group you want to lose is your most active. A tactic that could work for you is to serve them the ask via a promoted social media post.

ENGAGE

"To engage with ads can be about fundraising which is literally transactional.

But you can also use ads to deepen the connection to your organization and participation with the issues you care about."

Perhaps you are starting a new campaign or talking about a new issue and want to orientate an active audience to it. If it is important to you to foster a good relationship with a group you've invested in forming, consider sharing content with them and track whether or not it reaches them via paid ads.

Maybe you have folks on your list or following you on social media that aren't particularly active. You can think about testing different rounds of social media content with them to raise a connection. It could be sign-ups and petitions if you want to get them to make a firm commitment to an issue or type of engagement. Or it could be content in the form of a blog post or video if you think a more significant issue connection or knowledge is what is added to move them.

Goals for Tracking Impact

We now have some broad framework to think of audiences including appealing to new audiences, reconnecting with an old cohort and deepening engagement with an existing group.

Now let's talk about how to think about goals to make sure your ads have the impact you intended.

CONVERSION GOALS

Conversion goals are often the easiest to quantify and validate ad spending. These are goals that lead to direct online action. That action could be a donation, signing a form, or some sort of online petition. These kinds of goals work great when you know precisely the type of online conversion you are looking for.

The next question to ask is, what is it worth? This can be a lot less straightforward and takes some internal thinking. What are you—as an organization— willing to pay for a petition signature of someone entirely new to the list? Is there an active petition that you need to reach a target goal to pressure a target? In this case, what is it worth to get current list subscribers to sign on? Is it more valuable for early names to show momentum or later names to get across the finish line or both?

FEEDBACK

"Digital ads should be about goals, feedback, and moving something specific with ROI. Many areas of campaign and nonprofit work can get fuzzy. Ads should not. Your staff or contractors should be able to give clear numbers and data."

Sometimes people confuse new email sign-ups to their lists for their target audience and don't factor in the cost for the list they want. While it might make sense to get a decently targeted general list, if you want people to take a very specific action, you should figure out what that's worth to you.

Case Study: Expensive Sounding Sign-Ups

During the Obama 2012 campaign, we were exhausting our list for new recruits to our fellowship program. I had been working with our training team, led by Sara El-Amine, on how to optimize the sign-up forms and plans for recruiting. Working with the web development and analytics team, we were able to find the right volume of questions per page and the multi-step experience to increase people completing a reasonably lengthy application online.

Complete applications made it easier for staff on the ground to prioritize applicants who were serious. The barriers to entry, while very high by online standards, meant the staff with already limited capacity could work with a pool of applicants more committed to joining. Yet the barriers were not too high to dissuade people who were interested.

▶

After several successful rounds of emails and social media promotions, we realized most states were off of their goal of recruited fellows.

I approached the internal ads team to figure out an ads strategy. They were reluctant because the cost was likely to be prohibitive. We ran a pilot in one state, and the results (with some optimization in language) was still coming in at about $10 per completed form. After the state worked through applicant outreach, they confirmed 1 in 10 to the program, meaning they had a $100 cost per qualified lead. Sounds expensive right?

It was an entirely reasonable rate. These ads allowed the team to hit their goals of fellows recruited. Those fellows, in turn, were going to learn about community organizing and be directly responsible for authentic voter engagement in their community. Empowering new organizers and reaching targeted voters crucial to the election was easily worth $100 per fellow. But we could have never answered that authentically without knowing how to look at the cost and value of our goals.

IMPRESSION GOALS

A slightly softer goal type is the impression goal. We all know branding works. There are even political campaign strategies to index how many pieces of content a voter needs to see before being swayed. With some variation from studies, some report seven touches via mail, phone, in-person or otherwise is all it takes. We know there is some sway from billboard effects on people, and studies on that vary.

Think of impressions as online billboards. If your content is clear and concise, an impression can be part of a larger engagement strategy. To measure, you need to be willing to let a campaign run and see if you can test with a cohort for a shift in behavior.

An example would be an ad you allow to run repeatedly to an audience in hopes of an impact at a later date. Not just hitting the audience once, but allowing for repeat impressions to lead to later action around a targeted issue.

IMPACT

"Every platform counts views and impressions differently. If that's part of the impact you are tracking, get real numbers from vendors."

VIEW GOALS

Sometimes the goal is to spread a message. Raw view goals may be exactly what you are looking for. It's important to note that different ad platforms count views in different ways. Make sure you are reporting on what you really want to be. This number will change over time, so confirm how many seconds into content a platform counts as a "view" for accurate data.

If you think education on an issue is key, view goals are a great metric for that. Think about what the audience you think is most important to view the content, and what the value of each view would be for you.

A tip about online video and especially paid views—the place where people drop-off from a video can be pretty telling about the content. Does the drop-off happen at a particular transition? Do they drop where the video switches from storytelling to heavy facts? Use this data to inform your content and how you want to develop it going forward, or consider editing and rerunning the ads.

Digital Ad Planning and Budgeting Tips

Here are a few tips to help you get the most out of your ad planning and maximize the impact of your budget.

ABT—Always Be Testing. You should always have variation in copy and imagery for ads you run. Test and see what performs best. This also goes for email subject line testing. Test the ads with part of the audience and then expand the audience on the one performing better.

Ads as social messaging test. Most social media ads platforms offer what is often called "dark posts." These are posts that don't show up in follower timelines and are only seen by those served ads or those who shared the imagery. This can be a great way to test messaging and see which resonates better with your audiences.

Keyword search on search engines is a prime opportunity for low hanging fruit. Someone already searching for your issue or organization is one click away from some sort of action. Make sure you are matching those searches to the action you want to engage them with.

Make the budget around your goal, not your goal around your budget. I recently heard an organization ask how voters can be registered with $2,000. Yes, they will get some sort of answer and many ad firms would just go ahead and help them spend that money. The questions should start with how many voters you want to register and how you build a budget from there.

Summary

We talked about how digital ads can impact your goals in very tangible ways. Digital ads can help you to connect to new audiences, reconnect with existing audiences and deepen connections. You now have some distinct ways to think about ad use and goals when it comes to conversions, impressions, and views. Developing goals that are thoughtful about audience, outcome, and budget will help create a digital plan that has a positive impact.

Stories and Studies

Presented by Amy Leaman, JD Bryant, and Salim Zymet.

Clarity and Accessibility are Keys to Organizing

AMY LEAMAN // Co-Founder and Creative Director, *C Street* // @cstreet_ca

We've been a digital agency for five years and there's a common problem we're always solving. Our clients are extraordinary field organizers whose creativity gets stalled when they try to translate what they do on the ground onto the web. In the 2015 election in Canada, Leadnow was organizing their members to vote against Stephen Harper in target ridings. On the ground they were organizing in local teams. Using NationBuilder, we helped them build in permissions for organizers in a snowflake model, deploying multiple leaders as hubs of organized groups. Logged in users were automatically districted when they signed up, and on the front end could immediately see a photo and contact info of their local captains and organizing leads. This let Leadnow devolve organizing to their local teams instantly, and put power back in the hands of their supporters. They built a volunteer network of 45 local teams and 5,500+ volunteers who had 51,500+ voter-to-voter conversations at the door and on the phones.

Five Tips for Getting the Most Out of Your Agency

JD Bryant // Digital Advertising Director, *270 Strategies* //
www.linkedin.com/in/jdbryant/

For many campaigns and organizations, it doesn't always make sense to recruit and hire a full-time, in-house digital advertising team. Instead, many groups choose to rely on agencies for their built-in expertise and execution capacity. If you're considering exporting your advertising dollars, get the most out of them with these five tips:

1. Budget to your goals

Don't make the mistake of budgeting for digital advertising based on the remainder you have in a spreadsheet, or worse—on the size of your consultant's next mortgage payment. Instead, run a collaborative budgeting process with your agency that starts with your goals, and ends with a realistic budget to help you accomplish them.

2. Set aside a slush fund

Unexpected news can turn into a windfall for a digital team prepared to respond rapidly. But, scraping budget together for a sudden paid media program can be challenging. Make sure you're ready by setting aside a flexible budget with your digital ads agency and use it to boost high-performing social content or promote new acquisition hooks in big moments.

3. Speak with a consistent voice

If you've tasked your digital advertising agency with developing ad creative, make sure it's consistent with your brand. Remember: When you start advertising online, chances are most of the people who see your ads will be interacting with your brand for the very first time. Make sure your digital ad sets the tone for the relationship you hope to build with the people you're targeting.

4. Understand your new audience

Regardless of whether you run a list-building, persuasion, or mobilization campaign, you'll draw new attention and activity with digital ads. Work with your agency to supply you with the data that helps you identify these new "hot leads" and develop a follow-up program (whether by an email or SMS welcome series, ad retargeting, or one-to-one social engagement) to pick up where the user's last interaction with your brand left off.

5. Ask for reporting

It's your money—you deserve to know how it's being spent. Ask your digital advertising agency for regular, transparent reporting on active digital advertising campaigns. The reports they give you should be readable by top-level stakeholders in your organization, and also allow your digital practitioners to dive deep and gain a detailed understanding of campaign performance.

Digital Volunteer Recruitment: Examining Two Presidential Campaigns (2012 & 2016)

SALIM ZYMET // Engagement Director, *Crowdpac* // @salimzymet

So much has changed since 2012 (our presidents, anyone?!) but many of the digital tactics used in presidential state campaigns have remained the same. This case study is meant to shed a light on how things changed, and how they stayed the same when it comes to state digital programs.

First, a quick primer on what state digital programs in 2012 and 2016 were responsible for:

- Telling the story of the campaign in their state
- Recruiting and engaging volunteers through the internet
- Voter contact and mobilization through the internet

While our focus didn't change, our technology certainly did. I'm confident we ran a smarter, more aggressive and more robust digital program in 2016—it's unfortunate the outcome of the election didn't reflect our improved program.

Here's what didn't change for the most part:
- **Video.** Video was super important in 2012 and 2016, and we just put out much more of it in 2016. Both campaigns featured beautiful vignettes of supporters, candidates at rallies, and plenty of state-specific b-roll.
- **Storytelling.** Ultimately, we were storytellers. Though the story we told in

2012 more effectively moved the populace, my team ultimately told more powerful stories in 2016 than 2012. In 2012, we pretended to adopt a Humans of New York-esque flavor to our storytelling, but we nailed that in 2016. That wasn't a difference of intent or tactic, but rather a difference in understanding the benefit of super high-quality content and investing in camera equipment and talented writers to make that a reality.

- **Content.** As blogging died down generally, so too did our blogging in 2016. In 2012, each state had their own state-based blog to tell stories of supporters, in 2016, we mostly did that through Twitter, Facebook, Instagram, and Snapchat. We did have state-based web hubs, but storytelling was left to social media. I'd consider this a non-change, since we kept storytelling, just on different avenues.

- **Scope.** Ultimately, state programs were kept away from fundraising, digital ad strategy, and big-budget digital programs in 2012 and 2016. We focused on integrating with the rest of the state-based teams and recruiting volunteers through free tactics.

Here's what did change:
- **Data.** Our data architecture in 2016 was a lot better than in 2012, mostly due to advances other platforms had made, and the tech team in Brooklyn ensuring data sync between platforms was a high priority. While we scratched the surface of this towards the end of 2012, 2016 ended the siloed digital, field, and voting data for state digital teams, and it must stay that way.

- **Digital organizing.** We did this a lot better in 2016! Organizing directors and programs were all ears on how to use email, social media, text messaging to recruit and retain volunteers. Most states, including Ohio, had organizing directors and digital directors in locked arms, building a program of shared tactics to win their state. Though the outcome didn't show it, we made tremendous strides towards integrating digital into how state campaigns are ran and won. In many ways, we strived to make local organizers "digital directors" of their turf. We even regionalized our digital program, and I was able to bring on four digital organizers to cover various areas of Ohio to help on-the-ground organizers maximize their digital efforts.

- **Integrated departments.** It wasn't just organizing. From communications to political, voter protection to operations, digital was better integrated into each department so we could fill gaps, amplify opportunities, and help win.

- **Bye bye, vanity metrics.** In 2012, we were often distracted by reach, page likes, and page visits. Though metrics that are worth tracking, we did not have great systems for tracking conversions (people who actually show up and do things!), other than recruiting for Obama rallies. We didn't track how effectively we recruited or engaged volunteers. We did in 2016, thanks to an integrated approach with the data team.

It's interesting to look back on 2012 and see how much has changed, and how much has stayed the same. I hope eager campaigners have found this case study useful as they lay the groundwork for 2018 and 2020 campaigns.

DATA AND ANALYTICS

I always say good digital is a mix of creative art and hard science. Data and analytics are the hard science part. The science side allows you to monitor and see how your creative work is interacting and engaging with people.

Let's walk through a number of important pieces of data analytics to have a solid grasp of some best practices to make your digital planning solid. Knowing site analytics and some basic ways to make good decisions with that data is crucial. We'll dive into email analytics, using data well, and building out a smart data library. Then we will talk about social media analytics and the difference between vanity metrics and deeper engagement metrics. We'll wrap up with some tips to help you make the most of your Data and Analytics.

How to use this chapter

Non-Digital Leadership or Management: Data and analytics can help you understand what is happening in a program but only if the data is good and if it helps paint a picture.

Digital/Tech staffers: Practical knowledge for you as you grow and start to manage your own team.

New Staff/ Activists: Worth a look if you are joining a new team.

- Understanding the basics of website analytics
- Strategic thoughts for decisions based on analytics
- Understanding what conversions and sourcing are and how to use for planning
- Understanding of the fundamentals and difference between email, website, and social media analytics

Site Analytics

Websites are still the backbone of most organizations and campaigns wishing to maintain relationships with supporters online. Yes, you may engage and community build on social media platforms. But the place where you can deeply build supporter data and knowledge depth, is on your website.

Site analytics help you learn a lot of things about supporters. I highly recommend setting up Google Analytics. It's free, well documented, and very extensive. We'll approach this section from the framework of Google Analytics. Feel free to use whatever platform you prefer, but we will be discussing Google Analytics because of its accessibility.

PAGE ENGAGEMENT

Understanding site traffic helps you make better plans for where to prioritize your efforts and how to change your plan for engaging with people. It's important to understand your overall site traffic and what pages people currently engage with. Look at what pages are getting the most traffic. Does it line up with the pages you planned to promote via email, social, media and ads? If not, where are people coming from?

Is the amount of traffic you are getting on pages worth the investment in time on that page? A good way to think about this is if you are getting 20 to 30 page views a month on a page, is it worth prioritizing an overhaul? The answer might be yes if that's a page major donors often use. But the answer might be no if it was the download page for a flyer you thought hundreds of people would use.

It is also important to know about exit and bounce rates because a lot of traffic to a page can look good, but if the bounce or exit rates are high, that means people either didn't find what they were looking for or you didn't provide them with a next step. Bounce rate means they entered the site on that page and then just left. Exit rate means they were on at least one (if not more) pages before they decided to leave your site.

More often than not, sites have the most traffic on the pages with content you promote most on social media, email, and digital ads. You should dig in and see if your traffic lines up with that. Are there some outlying pages that are performing exceptionally well? What can you learn from those pages? There are many ways to interpret exit and bounce rates and being aware of these rates will help you to make more informed decisions.

Decisions Based on Analytics

While at Rainforest Action Network, we went through rebuilds of the website to solve for a variety of problems. In the second rebuild, we made conscious decisions to include as many things as possible on the homepage. This certainly flies in the face of prevailing winds of minimalism, but what we were trying to solve for was actually internal friction.

Knowing that most site traffic to date was flowing in from digital ads, email, and social media, I didn't have a high priority for overly focusing on the homepage. I wanted it to be thoughtfully orienting to new visitors, but did not want to spend as much time refining it as much as we would for the high traffic page types. But the digital team was likely to spend disproportionate amounts of time fielding requests to include things on the homepage. To avoid that, we planned to load up the homepage with everything someone might be looking for. There were some bugs in how some of the content was featured, but that's not why we chose to recreate the homepage.

IMPACT

"You can't know if your traffic is having the impact you want if you don't have goals or aren't tracking your analytics in any way."

After three months of consistent data checking, we were actually getting a lot of site traffic through the homepage. It seemed to have a strong correlation to the new user traffic from ads and our increased work with SEO and Google AdWords. Looking more closely at the traffic, however, it was a scattershot of pages people went to next, and we weren't getting them onto pages with priority information.

We took that data and endeavored to recreate a better homepage that included more orientation to the organizational content. We were more thoughtful on the amount of ease people would have to find the latest (and organizationally deemed most important) information. Had we not used data to make the decision, we may have just cleaned up the page and kept the "everything on the homepage strategy," but we couldn't ignore the amount of valuable traffic we were losing to the scattershot of next pages. We instead were able to make a well-informed series of decisions about what to feature for people to transition them to valuable engagement to move our goals forward.

CONVERSIONS AND SOURCING

One of the features I love about Google Analytics is setting up conversion goals. Essentially, you are setting up systems to see how many people who visit a page take a targeted action. You can set it up for a wide range of activities like signing a form or petition, making a donation, and downloading or engaging with a piece of content. Conversion goals empower you to know if the audience you are getting to the page took the actions you wanted to get there. If you have a reasonable email list size and petitions are important to you, and you increase conversion percentage by just a few percentage points, you may be adding thousands of engagements. Similarly, if you actively send a lot of fundraising asks, generating a better conversion rate in donations could lead to thousands of dollars a year.

A wonderful way to even more deeply understand conversions and engagement on a page, is to set up sourcing. Sourcing allows you to know how traffic arrived to your site, down to the exact page it comes from. You can set it to be pretty granular with the data down to an individual piece of social media content level and it can help you identify which piece of content brought in the traffic and engagement on the site. I would encourage you to dig in online or ask a sourcing specialist to help you come up with a system that works for you.

SOURCING FOR GROWTH PLANNING

While supporting the Nevada state staff for Obama 2012, we were working heavily on event building and there were going to be heavy rounds of surrogates in the state. I was sent in to help triage the state's digital program for the last 10 weeks of the campaign.

The state's social media numbers were pretty small—one of the many reasons I was sent in. But when I looked at the sourcing for how people were signing up for events in Nevada, it was clear to me that a large portion was from social media. That set in motion a plan to bolster social media growth with a focus on using it for event turnout. We were able to make gains in growth and the overall percentage of event attendees sourced to social media went up in correlation.

Email Analytics and Your Database

Core to so many organizations, projects, and campaigns functioning well, is a healthy email program. That's covered in that section called email. To make the most of your email program, you need to be aware of analytics and testing. There are the basic email tests like the subject line test which is ideally used for every email send. In every subject line test, you should look at open rate, click rate, action, unsubscribe, and spam.

Open rate is a good barometer of whether or not a small piece of content contains a subject line that connects with people. If your open rates are lower than you expected, it could be worth considering another test or two.

Click rate and action rate are prime indicators of whether or not the content in the email tracked with the subject line. It also shows if the email content was compelling enough for your audience to engage in the ask. **Unsubscribe rates** are another way to understand if your content was what people expected when they signed up.

Testing can, and ideally should, take broader looks beyond individual email analytics. You can see over time how cohorts of people behave based on their past engagement with you. Think about tests to see if certain sender names have different connections for people over time. One of the most important things about testing is understanding how your data changes over time because it will help you identify useful trends related to your website and audience. If you wanted to know if people on your list truly prefer email on Sunday or Wednesday, you will need to run that study over time. You should find ways to control for similar pieces of content.

I've seen a number of people "test" fairly significant things just once or twice—such as day or time of an email send—and make bold predictions from it. Yes, that is technically a test, but it isn't a very valid test. I also recommend testing again over time. What holds true today may be different in 6-12 months. If you use smart, well-designed tests, you'll be able to make smart informative plans.

To do this kind of testing, you'll need a good database, and you'll need to put information in there. It's important to ask yourself what kind of information you would like to know about your supporters to create better email preferences. If you don't have the answers today, can you start building out that data? Are there certain elements of data that your database inherently captures? For the data it doesn't capture, you will want to create a system of tags that you can assign to people based on interest and behavior. If your database doesn't allow for that, seriously consider migrating.

Unless you have a person just focused on data, I highly recommend minimizing the number of databases you use. Every migration back and forth is likely to cause errors. A number of times over the years, even on high functioning teams, I've seen data imports forgotten or messed up. Each import is a chance for error and probably an operational cost you haven't budgeted time for so take some time to do the research, consider your goals and choose wisely.

Data Library

Like all good libraries, a data library helps you stop and make sense of things. Far too many times, I've seen organizations start making tags for different information in their database and rely on institutional memory to know what each meant. Even the ones created by current staff members often forget the nuance of the tag originally created. I highly recommend creating an online spreadsheet that everyone shares.

In the spreadsheet, make very clear what each tag means. Creating a tag hierarchy and similar structures for similar actions and events will also help you to maintain consistent data that is easy to interpret.

MASTER ISSUES VS. SUB CAMPAIGNS

Let's say you work on Water Issues, Poverty Issues and a few that overlap. For the water-focused campaigns, you might assign something like Water_Access to people who signed up for things related to water access and Water_Clean_Flint for people concerned about the campaign for clean drinking water in Flint.

If you were hosting events, you might consider adding codes to abbreviate types of events so you could see who attended or signed up for a particular event. It might be an additional tag, and you would add that to your library like PB for phonebook or PC for press conference. That might look like Water_Clean_Flint_PB or PB_Flint depending on the structures that make the most sense for you.

A good data library over time will help you know your audiences better and make more accurate decisions when drafting plans.

FEEDBACK

"For long-term feedback, a data library is crucial. It can help you understand and tell a deep story of engagement."

Social Media Analytics

Data varies wildly based on the social media platform being used. For example, Facebook is a more sophisticated, very data-rich platform whereas Instagram is very limited. The important thing to figure out is what metrics matter to you and why. There are a number of articles on vanity metrics which include social media likes and basic reach, and while I agree with them on some levels, I think they undervalue some key pieces of engagement.

The number of Likes and Followers you have matters. Those things are a measure of potential reach and social validation. It's also hard (nearly impossible) to have meaningful numbers of conversions on a petition with only 100 Facebook likes. So if you are just getting started, ignore the folks that say all that matters is conversions from the content. You probably don't have that kind of capacity. Good content—meaning content people engage with via shares, likes and retweets—is the only thing that will bring you conversions later.

If you have capacity, then by all means, dig in and do research on which content is resonating with people. If you figure outsourcing, you can actually look at which tweet and Facebook posts drive sign-ups on petitions or attendance for events.

Data and Analytics planning is all about which numbers are going to move your big goals. Take some time and understand them. Good data should enable you to better prioritize and plan around what happens on your site, across email and social media platforms, so they all consistently tell a story about your work.

Learning frameworks for analyzing your data is easier now more than ever. Take a moment and dig into the plethora of free courses out there on analytics. Understand what is behind your numbers and be authentic about when you do and don't know what they say. I've watched a number of people misinterpret what a particular social media's post reach meant about a social media program at large. They didn't take the time to understand the mechanics of the platform and what kind of bigger trends were at play in the content. Had they had a stronger grasp of analytics and applied that lens, they would have seen a different and more accurate picture. This is similar for site content as well. If you are getting very few views, it is up to you to know if that is roughly the expected and maybe still valuable number, or if new strategy is needed.

Summary

Now you have a basic framework for ways to think about site traffic and using those numbers to make decisions. From those basics, you can dig into sourcing content and tracking conversions on your site so you can answer more finely grained questions. You should now be able to talk about important top-line metrics for email like open rate, click rate, action, unsubscribe, and spam rates. We went deeper to make sure you understand good tagging and what quality testing could dig more deeply into. A good database is key to making any of that work and a data library is key to making sense of the information you are collecting. Cultivate deeper insights into social media analytics and know what sort of numbers to focus on depending on the stage of your project or campaign and the reality of resources. If you bring all of these different data outlooks together and use them to inform your work, you will inherently create stronger digital plans.

Stories and Studies

Presented by Kaili Lambe, Benjamin Simon,
and Amelia Showalter.

Using the Right Ask at the Right Time

KAILI LAMBE // Organizing Director // @Kaili09

Having experience from an electoral campaign, I believed phone numbers were the most important piece of data to collect when I first started in digital work. My first few months as an online campaigner, it practically hurt not to add a phone number field. "But we might need it!" I insisted, even after I learned—and saw data to back up the concept— that requesting extra information decreases action rates. Adjusting to the idea of what information matters and how to reach people took time. Now eight years later, as I'm once again using digital tools to connect with people for offline action, I am finding I need to remind myself when it's not only okay, but actually critical to add a field like phone number to a page. When people are already high on the ladder of engagement, or signing up for an in-person event, they are likely to give you more information, and you're also more likely to need it to do deeper organizing and continue to build the relationship.

Using Feedback to Guide Your Social Change Campaign

BENJAMIN SIMON // Director of Strategic Services, *Mobilisation Lab* //
@BenjaminSimon

The Mobilisation Lab is a global learning and collaboration network to equip progressive movements and leaders to adapt and thrive in the digital, people-powered era. A key aspect of that work is improving the way all of us in the social change world plan and implement campaigns so that those campaigns are much better grounded in the needs and motivations of the people we're trying to inspire to take action.

We developed the Campaign Accelerator process to enable this—and frequent feedback loops with key audiences is absolutely vital. Here are three ways we encourage folks planning campaigns to gather feedback throughout the campaign:

1. **Use Audience Insights to Ground Your Campaign**—Before generating any sort of campaign tactics, we encourage everyone on a campaign team to go and have open-ended conversations with people who we'd want to make sure are engaged in the campaign work. These conversations aren't about testing specific ideas or messages. Instead, they seek to gain insight into the needs and motivations these people feel around a given topic, to understand what's really driving them. We then aggregate the dozens of total conversations together and pull out key insights which can be used to help generate ideas that are grounded in what the team learned in their conversations.

2. **Prototype Your Ideas as Early And Often as Possible**—Once teams have a few ideas they've generated (based on the insights mentioned above), we quickly move them into a prototyping phase, where they build very rough, physical versions of their ideas and go back out into the world to test them with same people they talked to earlier. This can be anything from a storyboard with construction, a drawing of a webpage, a cut-up cardboard box, etc. They can then get direct feedback on their ideas, and go back and refine. This process can be repeated many, many times, as teams home in on an ever-more-refined version of their campaign.

3. **Constant Adaptation Throughout**—Even once launched, campaigns should constantly be taking in feedback and using that feedback to update both strategy and tactics. What effects are your activities having? Do those effects alter your understanding of the area in which you're campaigning? Do they indicate some way in which you should shift either your tactics (to have greater impact) or your strategy (due to a better sense of how the system you're campaigning to shift actually works)?

One campaign we worked with involved engaging tech workers in a social change effort. The first step listed here—audience insights—was absolutely vital. The campaign team knew that tech workers were important, but viewed them as very different and foreign from themselves. In the interview prep, one of their questions was "how do you make friends?" But when the answer turned out to be "just like anyone else," and those interviews were combined with the rest of the team's, they learned that most tech workers really want to make a difference, they just aren't always sure how to do so.

And those feedback loops are fed through action—whether that's learning from campaign activities later on, or by seeking insight and feedback before you've even really figured out what you're doing. (Source: http://feedbacklabs.org/blog/using-feedback-to-guide-your-social-change-campaign/).

Accidental Tests Pay Off

Amelia Showalter // Co-Founder and CEO, *Pantheon Analytics* // @ameliashowalter

When brainstorming ideas to test, I often look at my friends and family behave and theorize about the mechanisms that make them take particular online actions. For instance, back on the 2012 Obama campaign we had a staff fundraising contest, so I was trying to get my friends to donate through my personal page. To win the contest I just needed to have the greatest number of donations; dollar amount didn't matter. So I asked all my friends to give the minimum, which was $3. Instead, I noticed that they were all giving $10. This was because the smallest button amount on the donation page was $10, and my friends didn't want to bother writing $3 into the "other amount" box. They just clicked on the $10 button.

This inspired me to run a test with our large email list, particularly with subscribers who had never donated before. In our emails we were asking them for $5, and then landing them on a page where the smallest button amount was also $5. We ran a test where we varied the email ask ($3 versus $5 versus $10) and also varied the smallest button ($5 versus $10). The winning combination was rather familiar to me: we got the most money by asking people for $3 in the email and then landing them on a page with a $10 button (though they could still write in other amounts). Our theory for why this works is that the $3 ask is low and friendly, so it gets more people to click onto the donation page. Then, when people are there on the page, it turns out most don't really mind giving $10. We actually later increased the smallest button amount to $15 after running a similar test.

I'm grateful that my friends' behavior was able to inspire all these rounds of testing. It was a big help to the campaign, and a good reminder to always observe what's going on around you and try to come up with testable theories. (And by the way, I won that staff fundraising contest—the prize was a phone call from Barack Obama to my mom).

DIGITAL ORGANIZING

Digital Organizing is my passion because good digital organizing is about understanding all of the facets that make up the sphere of digital strategy. Implementing thoughtful strategy can be used to engage, empower, and impact your goals.

I've seen the term digital organizing thrown around in very loose terms, especially in regards to what it means for staff and what they do. So we'll start this chapter on how to frame and think of digital organizing as a concept and a role. From there we'll dig into ways to think about supporter-based digital organizing, then we'll expand out to partner organizing. This chapter will close with some final thoughts on organizing principles to make the impact the world needs you to make.

How to use this chapter

Non-Digital Leadership or Management: Beyond marketing, having a static website, or broadcasting your message, digital organizing is the leveraging of the internet and technology for your campaign or cause. It might not be a fit for you, but you should have an understanding of digital organizing to make a decision.

Digital/Tech Staffers: Too often, people get stuck in execution of the disciplines in digital, and don't think about the humans they can be moving. Digital organizing is deeper-level human engagement. Even if it isn't a focus of your organization, it is worth understanding.

New Staff/Activists: If you are an activist, you should understand this. If you are a new staffer it is worth understanding.

KEY TAKEAWAYS AND ELEMENTS:
- This chapter digs into what exactly digital organizing is and is not
- How to leverage digital organizing for causes and to build community
- Strategy to intentionally build community or to leverage existing community
- Tips for organizing with partners
- Deeper digital organizing thoughts and principles

What is Digital Organizing?

I think of Digital Organizing as the online manifestation of community organizing. Community Organizing as defined by Google is, "the coordination of cooperative efforts and campaigning carried out by local residents to promote the interests of their community."

BRAINSTORM AND PLAN

"If you're really doing Digital Organizing, it should be at the forefront of all of your Brainstorm and Planning phases.

If it's always an afterthought, you are most likely missing opportunities for real engagement."

Digital Organizing is about using the internet to either bring together a community or leverage the internet for a community already working together.

I've heard of a few people reference the role of Digital Organizer by describing tasks rather than a vision for the role. Sometimes it is a set of tasks that support traditional field organizing, like supporting event creation and data. I would caution calling that role digital organizing and would liken it more to Organizing Support. Someone in that role may not be endeavoring to actually organize themselves. Other times I've heard the role referenced to someone who is sending emails. Well, that too sounds more like an email campaigner. Understanding how to apply the term "Digital Organizer" appropriately will help you to clarify your goals for your digital plan.

A Digital Organizer should be either building community or helping others leverage online tools to win campaigns. Online community can occur in a number of ways including forums, email lists, and listservs, and even around social media channels. What makes digital organizing specifically descriptive is that it is less about the tasks of digital tools and more about the how. The how of digital organizing is often about relationships between a cause and its supporters. Strategically cultivating online communities should involve intentionally building relationships and utilizing community power to work together in a coordinated way for a coordinated cause. That is the role of a Digital Organizer.

Digital Organizing for Causes and Community

Online community can take many forms. As mentioned above, it can form in forums, email lists and listservs, around social media channels, or in intentionally created community building spaces and groups online.

Healthy online communities have norms which make the purpose of the group clear, describe how to get invited and (to some degree) who is welcome. Good organizing doesn't mean everyone has to be invited, which also means it is okay to ask or help the trolls to leave. Just like in-person community dynamics, we make clear what commitments are, and the expectations for how members of the group should conduct themselves.

Sometimes community is entirely organic and self-organizing. But if you are reading this book, you have goals and things you want to impact in the world. Good digital organizing can help you meet those goals as long as you are intentional about what you want and how you are going to get there.

COMMUNITY IN FORUMS

My first paid online work was for a company that developed fantastic Miami-based travel, tourism, and local information called, MiamiBeach411.com. I was first drawn to the forums as I was relocating to Miami, and I appreciated the real dialogue about life and support in Miami. The website also created great localized information and content, which is where my first online writing appeared. There was a true community-based vision created by the founder Gus Moore.

The site itself is still an amazing model for developing and moderating great local information and online community. We see such behavior across the internet and often take it for granted, such as group sourced tech support on pages like Apple.com and Amazon.com. The reason online interaction works well in all of these places because of clearly set rules of conduct on how to engage, and clarity on who is a moderator with definitions on how things are moderated.

The early years of the Obama campaign were also host to online forums that allowed for great organizing. Now, I understand that forums can be troubling and difficult but you also don't have to build your own. Do you have an authentic connection to Reddit

Forums or other places on the internet? There is a lot of benefit for helping a self-moderated forum grow into the activists and ambassadors for your cause.

INTENTIONALLY BUILT COMMUNITY

The Call Tool. During the 2012 campaign a great example of Digital Organizing you probably haven't heard much about is the Call Tool team. Sometimes naming simplicity is best.

ENGAGE

"Intentional community doesn't happen. It is driven by real decisions and time. You will likely have to find a variety of ways to engage until it sticks.

It happens at every organization."

It was managed by Bridget Halligan who managed both the tech production of the call tool and building an online community to engage around the tool.

The tool itself would be deployable by state staff as a remote calling device for local volunteers and as the centerpiece of a national Call Tool team. But from experience, the campaign knew that building an all online community could lead to big results that impacted voter engagement goals. The manager went to great lengths to connect with volunteers who would become leaders. She invested time in building community and team identity. Most importantly she made the goals of the teams clear and held people accountable.

Digital Organizing isn't just about building community. It should be about impact and reaching goals. This program had its ups and downs from data to function issues like all programs do. Even its share of community issues. But staying focused meant reaching more voters than would have been reached with just local state work or by just emailing alone.

LEVERAGING EXISTING COMMUNITY

Sometimes digital organizing isn't about building new community online but is all about leveraging your existing community by augmenting their experience. This can appear in a number of ways, like building out new tools or locating digital resources for the community. It can also be training your current community on online tools to make their work more efficient or impactful.

Locating or building out the right tools should take two main questions into account:
1. What do you need the community to impact?
2. What does the community need in order to make that impact?

To answer these questions you need to know what your goals and expectations are for the community. Then you need to listen. Don't just listen to every request, but also look for the underlying themes. Knowing your own goal should be fairly straightforward. Listening for what is truly needed requires a more nuanced approach.

The reality is, like all good organizing, you have to make some hard decisions. When asking people what they broadly want, you might get an overwhelming list of features that would be cost prohibitive to buy or build. You might also hear a lot of things that are "nice to haves" instead of "need to haves" to accomplish the goal. Nuanced listening is understanding if people understand the current resources. It might be more of a training issue than a features issue. Either way, you are the best one to interpret the data and make a decision that gets you closer to what you want.

TRAINING ON THE TOOLS

During the 2012 campaign cycle I developed a wide range of trainings for digital staff, field staff, and volunteers. At the core of all of it, was empowering people to more effectively meet their goals and get President Obama another term in office. The trainings ranged from technical aspects of digital jobs, to social media for day-to-day organizing, to how to leverage campaign-built tools to augment traditional organizing.

The campaign's "Dashboard" organizing platform had many fits and starts. Or starts and fits. I had the privilege of working through a rolling series of trainings with the project managers, Jessica Morales Rocketto and Jeff Gabriel. It was a piece of technology meant to unify systems and make the overall experience for organizers better. For many of the early users, I thank you still. We learned training by training, and from launch successes and setbacks, how to make things better. However, some of those setbacks made a fair share of supporters hesitant to use the tools because at a small scale, their current hacks around the previously broken system were working. I knew a thing or two about that.

When I was a field organizer for Obama '08 no-one had showed me the value of marking volunteers for their shifts in the database and when you had only three or four consistent volunteers, it didn't matter. As the campaign escalated, we needed to confirm and manage volunteers better. It easily clicked since we had data on who had done what in the past and that made it easier to prioritize who to call back for what. It changed our world and ability to hit, then exceed, goals.

I took that knowledge and worked with more senior organizing leadership. I laid down the value and got their buy-in. From there we got the buy-in of other levels of leadership, and the trainings met far less resistance. It was organizing the organizers to help the other organizers more effectively do their work. Yes, very meta and a great example of how approaching even digital training as an organizer, you see that empowerment has an exponential effect.

DIGITAL ORGANIZING WITH PARTNERS

Digital tools have allowed us to amplify and spread messages like never before. In an instant, an issue hashtag can be trending, a video can gain thousands of views, and an image can become a meme. When done well, it is rarely a fluke. More often than not, there was a plan that crossed between good strategy and good digital organizing.

Sometimes when we are organizing community we are organizing a community of communities. It is not just leveraging one immediate network, but thinking about how can you work in a way the leverage multiple entities' online presence. When working this way, you should always keep in mind what would make the ask easiest for you if you were the one being asked for something.

Keep the ask clear and consistent. Are you asking for groups to join for one particular day or action, or a longer-term commitment? Be sure to ask yourself if you could build a better long-term relationship by asking for everything up front or by having one successful day that others would want to be part of in the future. There isn't one right answer but you should be thoughtful about what you need and want both in the short and long-term plan for your community.

Try to package things in as simple of a system as possible. Remember that every barrier you set between the content and whoever needs to grab and schedule it, the less likely it is to happen. If you have a really clear goal and the partners are needed to get there, then make that clear. We all respond better to knowing how we can be directly impactful.

DIGITAL ORGANIZING THOUGHTS AND PRINCIPLES

Model what works well in person when you can and decide where it makes sense. Does your organization or campaign have chapters? Then make sure your replicate and respect that structure online.

Are there founding principles and ideas to your organization that people connect to? If yes, make sure you replicate those principles in online community with your language and behavior.

Don't fear the small ask. Sometimes people are afraid to make a small ask for fear of losing a supporter. This ask could be to share content or change their profile image. If you've built a meaningful relationship with someone, it is really about the right ask, at the right time, to the right audience. I've met a few major donors over the years that loved when we asked them to tweet. It allowed them to leverage their social clout (Klout) and gave them another way to engage with a cause they loved when their schedule didn't allow for anything else.

Empower people where you can. Most people thrive with respect and responsibility. Let them and your organization thrive.

At the end of the day, good digital organizing is just good organizing online using online tools. The human element still applies and is what impacts change.

Digital organizing and the role of a digital organizer is all about intentionally building relationships and leveraging community power to work together in a coordinated way for a coordinated cause. You can use digital organizing to build a new online community. It is also about leveraging your existing community or augmenting their experience. You can and should approach coordinating groups with a human-centric organizing model. Good digital organizing will help you execute your plans and meet your goals to make the impact the world needs you to make.

Summary

Digital organizing is an online expression of community organizing—the coordination of cooperative efforts to promote a shared interest/cause. Though there are many tasks and tools involved in being a digital organizer, it's more about vision and focus on goals. The best digital organizers know how to intentionally build meaningful relationships and leverage existing communities.

Stories and Studies

Presented by Mark Crain, Jess Morales Rocketto, and Jeff Gabriel.

Reach Out and Follow Up

MARK CRAIN // Mobile Innovation Director, *MoveOn.org* // @markscrain

I ran issue campaigns at MoveOn.org, one of the largest progressive advocacy organizations in the country for four years before being tapped to build out our mobile program. Our task? Give members the best campaign experience possible from their mobile devices and use new mobile technology to drive more actions. As the 2016 election approached it was clear that text-based GOTV was going to be a major program for many campaigns and independent organizations—it probably wasn't the most unique value-add our members could bring to the table. Instead, we decided to bolster our field program by texting to recruit members to neighborhood canvasses.

We knew this would help our total numbers—but we had no clue texting would lead to 40% of our sign-ups. So what were the key takeaways? First, a texting program opens itself to an entirely different volunteer base than your typical door knockers or callers—introverts ftw! Second, texts can be intrusive, but in a high-energy, high-stakes moment, most recipients will forgive you for making the ask. Third, a commitment over a text is indeed a softer commitment than over the phone or by face—be prepared to remind and follow up if you want to keep your show rate up. A strong texting program is well-targeted, has committed texters, doesn't bombard or abuse the recipient, and establishes an ongoing, responsive conversation.

Diversity Investment in Digital Organizing

JESS MORALES ROCKETTO // Political Director, *National Domestic Workers Alliance* // @JessLivMo

To say that we had an uphill battle incorporating digital organizing into Hillary for America would be an understatement. By the end of 2016, we had built a juggernaut of a program that has lots of lessons for a path forward for Democrats who want to use digital on their campaigns. I'll never forget learning that our campaign manager didn't even think "digital organizing" was real.

Our goal was extremely different than either Bernie Sanders in the primary or Trump in the general—their programs were all about big. Big crowds, big Reddit threads, big organizing. We took the complete opposite strategy and built something that mirrored old-fashioned community organizing as closely as possible, and always prioritized the one-to-one interaction. Hillary was the candidate for an intimate backstage meet and greet or a small coffee meeting, so we were the program that prioritized peer-to-peer conversations.

Our team believed deeply in the power of combining our digital prowess not just to make it easier for organizers and volunteers to complete tasks, but to make it easier for them to connect and have the conversations that win elections. And this informed every level of our program—from our first-ever digital voter hotline that answered 600,000 voters questions in real time on social platforms, to the 40 million peer-to-peer text messages that we sent for every piece of our program.

It would be hard for me to highlight the full scope of our work, but here are some major highlights so you can get a small inkling:

- Hired a diverse team of 99 in HQ and 14 battleground states
- Recruited over one million volunteers
- Sent 40 million peer-to-peer text messages in a first of its kind voter engagement program
- Grew a 1.2 million subscriber SMS list, raising $9 million and announcing Hillary's vice presidential pick
- Generated 5.8 million phone calls via our online call tool
- Generated hundreds of millions of social media impressions for National Voter Registration Day
- Registered over 200,00 voters online in key battleground states
Built battleground state digital programs in 14 states
- Recruited over 250,000 grassroots social media volunteers to drive our message on social
- Trained over 50,000 new volunteers, most of whom received their first campaign interaction through our program
- Answered 600,000 questions through our digital voter protection hotline

If you're running a campaign in 2018 or beyond, invest in digital organizing.

Campaigns are always ready to hire an email firm that raises money, and many are moving in peer-to-peer texting because it's a quick way to reach voters, but these aren't digital organizing programs. A digital organizing program is infused into every part of your program: recruiting social media volunteers to authentically communicate your message to their friends, a mobile program that combines broadcast and peer-to-peer SMS to meet voters where they are, and technology that makes it easy for people to find their polling place and make a plan to vote. It requires an early investment, like any good comms or field program, and it requires a commitment to creativity and flexibility.

We had to reach millions of voters, so our program was well-resourced and had almost 100 people. But one of the reasons I know this can work at any level of campaign or organization is that we didn't start out that way. From the campaign manager on down, we had to convince people that digital organizing deserved time, money, and people. When we started our SMS program, which eventually created an entirely new campaign spokesperson in "Jess from HFA," we had zero subscribers, no full-time staff dedicated to the program, and had spent most of our political capital to even get the program started.

That's an expensive risk that we had the resources to take, so let me talk about one that is less expensive. Tens of thousands of people signed up every week to volunteer for the campaign, and our team couldn't follow up with them in enough time to keep our hot leads warm. So we started a weekly new volunteer call and we invited anyone who had signed up on our email list in the last seven days, then we faithfully did it every single week until the end of the election. We answered every single question, followed up with every single email, and gave people action options they could take the very next day. This didn't require a huge resource investment—we made a deck, we scheduled it on our calendars, we worked with the email team to send it, and we held that time faithfully every week. We trained at least 50,000 volunteers this way, which is a conservative estimation.

One of the major reasons we were able to do this work is that we focused on hiring. By any measure, this was a tough sell—we hired approximately 50 people around the country in less than two months. Our team was incredibly diverse because we put a stake in the ground and we didn't hire unless we had a diverse pool of applicants. We sent to every listserv we could, we looked at the roster of every firm to poach people, and we sent emails to every single friend we could think of. And then my team spent hundreds of hours looking through the tens of thousands of resumes and looked especially for people who had "non-traditional" résumés and a passion for Hillary Clinton.

Lots of folks in progressive politics wring their hands about diverse hiring, but the real secret is: Hire diverse leadership. Generate a pool of résumés as big and far-reaching as possible. Prioritize hiring passionate hustlers who have the experiences of the voters you want to reach. Be willing to train people who are almost there with just a little push. And trust their instincts and expertise when they raise creative, exciting ideas that scare you a little.

In 2018, invest in digital organizing. We need it, and the results speak for themselves.

Tools and Tips for Digital Organizing

JEFF GABRIEL // Chief of Staff, *Common Sense Media* // @Jeff_Gabe

Can that product/platform/app win this campaign? The short answer is no, and be careful how much you invest your time, money and effort into that "silver bullet" product for political engagement tech. Now, that's not to say there are not a lot of helpful tools out there, but is that "tool" going to be the main reason you win an election or legislative win? Probably not.

I've worked on two presidential elections and on behalf of some of the largest issue advocacy organizations in the country, where I spent a lot of my time at the intersection of organizing, digital engagement, and technology. After working in the field for the Obama Campaign and OFA from 2008 through 2011, I was hired as a Product Manager to help provide a "field perspective" to the Presidential re-election campaign tools for the first ever in-house technology team based out of the National Headquarters in Chicago. I then became the Program Manager for the largest in-house custom built engagement platform called Dashboard.

Dashboard was a custom built campaign platform designed to solve the relatively new problem in organizing—the digital/field divide. Eventually, Dashboard became a platform where any campaign supporter could sign up to get involved by entering their address, which would then be matched to a custom turf assignment that was created and matched to a backend API that connected to the field tool platform, VoteBuilder. Once a supporter created an account and entered their home address, Dashboard then connected that supporter to their exact local neighborhood team and their team leader would be notified, and then could engage that new supporter in important volunteer work on behalf of the campaign. The new supporter/volunteer could also make calls, raise money, and or RSVP for their local team events. Voila, the digital organizing divide was bridged.

Ultimately, the goal was to move a supporter from online volunteering to offline organizing aka moving them up the proverbial "ladder of engagement." Dashboard and a newly developed backend API created a wave of trackable data and reports that funneled up through the campaign hierarchy from a supporter, to their neighborhood team, to their Field Organizer, to their Regional Field Director to their State Field Director, to their National Regional Director, to their National Regional Director, and finally, to The National Field Director.

If you would have told me when I was a Field Organizer in 2008 that such a platform existed, I would have laughed and wouldn't have believed you. All staffers and volunteers learned throughout the Obama organizing years that "if the data didn't exist it didn't happen." We were truly a national campaign that was people-centered, but data-driven. The fact that we were able to build a platform that could funnel supporters online to offline and make it all trackable without manual data entry required was an organizer's dream made into a reality.

In part because of this tool's insights, we were able to significantly increase the amount of time and duration that volunteers ended up working with our neighborhood teams across the country. By Election Day, we had over 340,000 users on this platform all with one goal: help get Barack Obama elected by turning out the vote.

All that said, the process, expectations, feature priorities, tool scope, and timing were painful to live through and not optimal. It wasn't all sunshine and lollipops. In fact, if you ask a lot of field staff from the 2012 campaign, they probably wouldn't agree with my assessment and they may have found Dashboard to be more cumbersome then it was worth. Why is that? Well, it turns out building custom technology platforms and connecting it via APIs to existing third-party campaign technology is really hard. Of course, building that kind of product is hard, regardless of the circumstance. But building a first-of-its-kind product in the throes of a Presidential campaign, with limited time and a ton of pressure? Almost impossible.

Especially, because like all custom products you need to iterate releases with new features and fix bugs on a weekly basis for an audience who doesn't have the time or where-withal to make it a priority. We were building to an audience who had truly unrealistic expectations of what this product was going to do (which was our fault) and how hard it was going to be to get a finished product in time for it to be truly helpful and effective. Ultimately, most of the state staff and volunteer organizers neither had the time nor experience dealing with a pre-beta tech. With a campaign that was constantly adding thousands of organizer and reassigning new turf, Dashboard didn't provide all the management tools needed in a fast-paced environment such as a Presidential campaign to service everyone within an extremely robust and ever-fluid campaign hierarchy. If that chain broke, there was going to be a problem with use, buy-in and how impactful this tool could be to our work and goals. Where Dashboard worked best? Frankly, it was the non-battleground states because they had more stable structures, less staff and needed a tool to leverage the influx of volunteers they had to plug into their local organizing activities.

From that experience, along with working for or on behalf of other national issue advocacy organization trying to bridge the digital organizer divide by building custom, I learned one thing: building campaign technology is really hard. And frankly, a mission I'm now leaving to other friends and colleagues to continue to solve. Below are the lessons I learned during my years in online organizing and campaign tech. I hope you find them helpful in your endeavors in trying to make the world a more just place.

- Set the right expectations for your key early adapters and business owners.
- Be realistic; limit the scope of what your tool is going to solve and not.
  - Is it a mobilization tool?
  - A management tool?
  - A communication tool?
  - A community engagement tool?
- Be careful about serving too many clients. Know what audience you're building

for and how it's going to help the rest of the organization or campaign.

- Technology is never to going to fix our political system or win a campaign. It's a tool that should help supplement the work you're already trying to build.
- Unless you have a very large budget and a lot of time, don't go build it yourself. Use a proven product.
- Build something that is mutually beneficial for all involved.
- Make sure you listen to your core users and get them to buy-in early. They're going to be your biggest ambassadors and they better see the value in what your building and how it will help them. Remember, they're the key gatekeepers.

Good luck out there. While nothing you build will ever be a silver bullet, I hope you build something that helps a movement forge ahead a little more boldly, efficiently, and authentically.

ABOUT THE AUTHOR

Brad A Schenck is a leading digital and engagement strategist for nonprofits and political campaigns. He's been driving engagement via the internet for over a decade.

By the mid 2000's, Brad was leveraging the internet to organize progressive documentary screenings and for community organizing projects. By 2007, he was producing freelance videos for nonprofits and for travel and tourism content in Miami.

In 2008 and 2009, he focused on electing President Barack Obama, driving community service, and helping pass Obamacare with Organizing for America. In 2010, he took on a role as a regional new media manager with OFA, and led the strategy to implement social media in the field as well as develop trainings. As part of the Democratic National Committee, he advised dozens of state Democratic Parties, as well as Senate, Gubernatorial, and Congressional campaigns.

This evolved into a position where Brad's multiple roles with President Obama's 2012 campaign included developing digital strategy for battleground states, and becoming the first Digital Training Program Manager (Director) in political campaign history. He was the lead developer of the first Digital Fellowship to be offered by a major political campaign. In his role, he developed training courses, webinars, and mentorship that developed thousands of volunteers and organizers, state digital directors, staff, and field staff.

After winning the election, Brad was asked to serve as Obama-Biden 2012 Inaugural National Day of Service's Digital Manager. He was able to build on the massive state-by-state system of volunteer content developers and managers to develop a nationally trending a conversation about service.

Loving all of the momentum this unprecedented network had built, Brad continued to serve the Obama movement as the founding Digital Strategist for Organizing for

Action(OFA). At OFA, he continued to develop training and mentorship for staff and volunteers, and helped the organization evolve from electoral campaigning to issue campaigning.

From 2014 to 2016, he rebuilt (from the ground up) the digital department for Rainforest Action Network, an international activism and advocacy organization. During that time he also supported the CREDO SuperPAC, driving the digital side of their field campaign.

During the 2016 cycle, he took on local and national issues, driving engagement for school board elections, ballot propositions, and local elections. All of that in the background while running groundbreaking registration and GOTV programs as Head of Engagement for Vote.org. Brad's work at Vote.org included running unprecedented tests with SMS for voter registration and turnout, and one of the largest non-presidential GOTV operations in the country.

In 2017, Brad launched the first edition of *The Digital Plan* and worked with a range of local and international organizations.

To kick off 2018, Brad launched The Digital Plan Community, an online training community, mentoring others in digital and tech for nonprofits and campaigns. All central to Brad's mission of scaling knowledge in the digital and tech fields that helps others win political campaigns, grow nonprofit organizations, launch projects, and meet goals.

ABOUT THE EDITOR

Katrina Mendoza is a video producer and digital marketer with a business that focuses on leveraging community partnerships to make a local impact through storytelling and strategic digital design.

She lives with her wife in Santa Fe, New Mexico, where they own *Ditch The Box Studios,* a design and video production company elevating local artists and community leaders. Some of their project highlights include:

- Fundraising for a digital fabrication program creating apprenticeship pathways for at-risk young adults.
- Launching a storytelling initiative to revitalize the South-side industrial arts district in Santa Fe.
- Directing the digital strategy for Santa Fe's diversity candidate in the race for Mayor.
- Providing female artists with mentorships and free promotional videos to amplify their reach.
- Successfully obtaining the honor of hosting (and now promoting) the Inaugural Nation of Makers conference in Santa Fe, June 2018.

As a techie-artistic mystic, Katrina is always looking for new collaborative projects, especially when they elevate and support community, diversity and the intersection between art and tech. She can be reached at k.alexandramendoza@gmail.com.

Made in the USA
Columbia, SC
19 July 2019